Non-Lea[...] [...]porters' Guide [...] [...]025

– [...] Clubs

EDITOR
John Robinson

Fourth Edition

British Library Cataloguing in Publication Data
A catalogue record for this book is available from the British Library

ISBN: 978-1-86223-534-2

72 St. Peter's Avenue, Cleethorpes, DN35 8HU, United Kingdom

Website www.soccer-books.co.uk
e-mail info@soccer-books.co.uk

Printed in the UK by 4edge Ltd

FOREWORD

It has been 18 years since we published the Third Edition of this Guide specifically for Step 3 Clubs so, needless to say, there have been lots of changes both for the clubs themselves and also to the overall structure of the Non-League Football Pyramid.

Also, although directions can now be obtained online via Google and Satnav (as can much of the information contained within this guide) it can take a great amount of searching and stress!

Our thanks go to the numerous club officials who have aided us in the compilation of information contained in this guide as well as Michael Robinson (page layouts), Bob Budd (cover artwork) and Tony Brown (Cup Statistics – www.soccerdata.com). We are particularly grateful to Rob Cavallini and Russ Cox (@RussWWFC on twitter) who have helped us greatly by supplying some of the ground photographs used in this book.

Readers who have up-to-date ground photographs which they would like us to consider for use in a future edition of this guide are requested to contact us at our address which is shown overleaf on the title page.

We would like to wish our readers a safe and happy spectating season.

John Robinson
EDITOR

CONTENTS

THE NORTHERN PREMIER LEAGUE PREMIER DIVISION

Website www.thenpl.co.uk

Clubs for the 2024/2025 Season

ASHTON UNITED FC

Founded: 1878
Former Names: Hurst FC and Rose Hill FC
Nickname: 'Robins'
Ground: Hurst Cross Stadium, Surrey Street, Ashton-Under-Lyne OL6 8DY
Record Attendance: 11,000 (1952)

Colours: Red & White striped shirts, Red shorts
Telephone Nº: (07866) 360200
Ground Capacity: 4,500
Seating Capacity: 250
Website: www.ashtonunited.co.uk
E-mail: secretary@ashtonunited.co.uk

GENERAL INFORMATION

Car Parking: Street parking only
Coach Parking: At the ground
Nearest Railway Station: Ashton (1 mile)
Nearest Bus Station: Ashton
Club Shop: At the ground
Opening Times: Before and during matches only
Telephone Nº: (07866) 360200

GROUND INFORMATION

Away Supporters' Entrances: No usual segregation

ADMISSION INFO (2024/2025 PRICES)

Adult Standing/Seating: £12.00
Concessionary Standing/Seating: £8.00
Under-12s Standing/Seating: £1.00 with a paying adult

DISABLED INFORMATION

Wheelchairs: Accommodated
Helpers: Please phone the club for information
Prices: Please phone the club for information
Disabled Toilets: Available
Contact: (07866) 360200 Please contact the club prior to the game to make necessary arrangements.

Travelling Supporters' Information:
Routes: From the M1: Exit at Juntion 35A and follow signs for Manchester A616. Follow A616 for 11 miles then turn left at roundabout towards Manchester on A628. Follow A638 for 14 miles, passing through Tintwistle and Hollingworth. At the first set of traffic lights at the Gunn Inn go straight on and up the hill for ½ mile. Bear right at the A6018 signposted Ashton-Under-Lyne, Stalybridge and Mossley. Follow for 3 miles, passing Stalybridge Celtic FC on the left. At the 4th set of traffic lights turn right just past the BP Garage. Continue up Ridge Hill Lane for 250 yards where the road bears left and becomes Darnton Road. Continue, passing boating lake and Hospital on the right. Continue through the lights signposted Oldham and go up the hill for ½ mile. * Turn left at the first set of traffic lights then immediately right for the ground; From the M60: Take M60 towards Stockport, exit at Junction 23 and turn left (signposted Ashton). After 100 yards turn right at traffic lights onto A635 towards Ashton. After ½ mile you will reach a roundabout with a Police Station on the left. Stay in the 2nd lane heading towards Stalybridge & Halifax (still A635). Go straight on at next roundabout with Asda on the right until the following roundabout. Take 2nd exit signposted A670 Tameside Hospital. After 500 yards turn right into Mossley Road and after 600 yards turn left at the traffic lights towards Oldham and continue up the hill for ½ mile. Then as from *.

BAMBER BRIDGE FC

Founded: 1952
Former Names: None
Nickname: 'The Brig'
Ground: The SFC Stadium, Brownedge Road, Irongate, Bamber Bridge, Preston PR5 6UU
Record Attendance: 3,250 (28th March 1992)

Colours: White shirts with Black shorts
Telephone Nº: (01772) 909695
Ground Capacity: 2,642
Seating Capacity: 499
Website: www.bamberbridgefc.com
E-mail: Use the contact form on the club's website

GENERAL INFORMATION

Car Parking: At the ground
Coach Parking: At the ground
Nearest Railway Station: Bamber Bridge (1¼ miles)
Nearest Bus Station: Preston
Club Shop: At the ground
Opening Times: One hour before kick-off on matchdays

GROUND INFORMATION

Away Supporters' Entrances & Sections:
No usual segregation

ADMISSION INFO (2024/2025 PRICES)

Adult Standing: £12.00
Adult Seating: £12.00
Concession/Student Standing: £8.00
Concession/Student Seating: £8.00
Note: Under-16s are admitted for £2.00 with a paying adult and Under-11s are admitted free with paying adult.

DISABLED INFORMATION

Wheelchairs: Accommodated
Helpers: Please phone the club for information
Prices: Please phone the club for information
Disabled Toilets: Available
Contact: (01772) 909695 (Bookings are necessary)

Travelling Supporters' Information:
Routes: Exit the M6 at Junction 29 and follow Preston signs to the major roundabout onto London Way. Take the 3rd exit at the next roundabout signposted Bamber Bridge. Take the 1st right and at the end of the road after 100 yards turn left into the ground.

BASFORD UNITED FC

Founded: 1900
Former Names:
Nickname: 'The Lions or The Ambers'
Ground: Mill Street Playing Field, Greenwich Avenue, Basford, Nottingham NG6 0LD
Record Attendance: 719
(vs Macclesfield FC 13/04/2024)

Colours: Amber shirts and shorts
Telephone Nº: (0115) 924 4491
Ground Capacity: 1,950
Seating Capacity: 300
Website: www.basfordunited.com

GENERAL INFORMATION

Car Parking: At the ground
Coach Parking: At the ground
Nearest Railway Station: Bulwell(1 mile)
Club Shop: At the ground
Opening Times: Matchdays only 2.00pm to 6.00pm

GROUND INFORMATION

Away Supporters' Entrances & Sections:
No usual segregation

ADMISSION INFO (2024/2025 PRICES)

Adult Standing: £11.00
Adult Seating: £11.00
Concession Standing: £8.00
Concession Citizen Seating: £8.00
Students & Under-16s Standing: £5.00
Students & Under-16s Seating: £5.00

DISABLED INFORMATION

Wheelchairs: Accommodated
Helpers: Admitted
Prices: Normal prices apply for the disabled but helpers are admitted free of charge.
Disabled Toilets: Available
Contact: (0115) 924 4491 (Bookings are not necessary)

Travelling Supporters' Information:
Routes: Exit M1 at Junction 26 and take the A610 to Nottingham for about 1.3 miles. Turn left at the 2nd roundabout onto Cinderhill Road following signs for Bulwell and continue for about 400m before turning right into Bagnall Road. After another 800m turn left into Greenwich Ave and the ground is straight ahead.

BLYTH SPARTANS AFC

Founded: 1899
Former Names: None
Nickname: 'Spartans'
Ground: Croft Park, Blyth, Northumberland, NE24 3JE
Record Attendance: 10,186 (1956)
Colours: Green and White striped shirts, Black shorts
Telephone Nº: (01670) 352373 (Office)
Ground Capacity: 4,435
Seating Capacity: 556
Website: www.blythspartans.com
E-mail: generalmanager@blythspartans.com

GENERAL INFORMATION

Car Parking: At the ground
Coach Parking: At the ground
Nearest Railway Station: Newcastle
Nearest Bus Station: Blyth (5 minutes walk)
Club Shop: At the ground
Opening Times: Matchdays only
Telephone Nº: (01670) 352373

GROUND INFORMATION

Away Supporters' Entrances & Sections:
No usual segregation

ADMISSION INFO (2024/2025 PRICES)

Adult Standing: £15.00
Adult Seating: £17.00
Senior Citizen Standing: £9.00
Senior Citizen Seating: £11.00
Ages 11 to 16 & Student Standing: £6.00
Ages 11 to 16 & Student Seating: £8.00
Note: Under-11s are admitted free of charge when accompanied by a paying adult.

DISABLED INFORMATION

Wheelchairs: 3 elevated wheelchair spaces available
Helpers: Please phone the club for information
Prices: Adult disabled fans are charged the Senior Citizen rate shown above. Younger disabled fans charged lower rate.
Disabled Toilets: Available adjacent to the Main Stand
Contact: (01670) 352373 (Bookings are necessary)

Travelling Supporters' Information:
Routes: Pass through the Tyne Tunnel and take the left lane for Morpeth (A19/A1). At the 2nd roundabout (after approximately 7 miles) take full right turn for the A189 (signposted Ashington). After 2 miles take the slip road (A1061 signposted Blyth). Follow signs for Blyth turning left at the caravan site. At the 2nd roundabout turn right and the ground is on the left.

FC UNITED OF MANCHESTER

Photo courtesy of John Mills @ Altius Photography

Founded: 2005
Nickname: 'F.C.'
Ground: Broadhurst Park, 310 Lightbowne Road, Moston, Manchester M40 0FJ
Record Attendance: 4,232 (29th May 2015)
Ground Capacity: 4,400
Seating Capacity: 750
Colours: Red shirts with White shorts
Telephone Nº: (0161) 769-2005
Website: www.fc-utd.co.uk
E-mail: office@fc-utd.co.uk

GENERAL INFORMATION

Car Parking: 160 spaces at the ground. Pre-booking only, £5.00 charge. Other car parks are located within ½ mile of Broadhurst Park. Check the club's website for further details.
Coach Parking: Phone the club on (0161) 769-2005
Nearest Railway Station: Moston (¾ mile)
Nearest Bus Station: A number of services travel to the ground. Please check the club's website for further details.
Club Shop: At the ground
Opening Times: Matchdays only
Telephone Nº: (0161) 769-2005

GROUND INFORMATION

Away Supporters' Entrances & Sections:
No usual segregation but away fans will be accommodated in the Lightbowne Road End if necessary.

ADMISSION INFO (2024/2025 PRICES)

Adult Seating: £12.00
Senior Citizen (Over-60s)/Student Seating: £8.00
Under-18s Seating: £3.00

DISABLED INFORMATION

Wheelchairs: Spaces for wheelchairs are available in all areas of the ground
Helpers: One helper admitted per wheelchair
Prices: Normal prices for wheelchair users. Helpers are admitted free of charge.
Disabled Toilets: Available behind the Main Stand
Contact: (0161) 769-2005 (Bookings are not necessary)

Travelling Supporters' Information: From the M60 travelling clockwise: Exit the M60 at junction 20 and turn onto the A664. At the traffic signals turn left onto the A6104. Travel straight on and then at the Greengate roundabout take the 4th exit onto Lightbowne Road, the B6393. Carry straight on for around a half a mile and Broadhurst Park is on your left; From the M60 travelling anti-clockwise: Exit the M60 at junction 22, then straight on to Hollingwood Avenue, the A6104 . Travel straight on and then at the Greengate roundabout take the 1st exit onto Lightbowne Road, the B6393. Carry straight on for around a half a mile and Broadhurst Park is on your left.

GAINSBOROUGH TRINITY FC

Founded: 1873
Former Names: Trinity Recreationists FC
Nickname: 'The Blues'
Ground: KAL Group Stadium, Gainsborough, Lincolnshire, DN21 2QW
Record Attendance: 9,760 (1948)
Colours: Blue shirts and shorts
Telephone Nº: (07500) 838068
Ground Capacity: 4,340
Seating Capacity: 504
Website: www.gainsboroughtrinity.com
E-mail: info@gainsboroughtrinity.com

GENERAL INFORMATION

Car Parking: Opposite the ground (£2.00 charge).
Coach Parking: Available by prior arrangement
Nearest Railway Station: Lea Road (2 miles) and also Gainsborough Central on Saturdays only (½ mile)
Nearest Bus Station: Heaton Street (1 mile)
Club Shop: At the ground
Opening Times: Matchdays only
Telephone Nº: (07500) 838068

GROUND INFORMATION

Away Supporters' Entrances & Sections:
No usual segregation

ADMISSION INFO (2024/2025 PRICES)

Adult Standing: £10.00
Adult Seating: £10.00
Concessionary Standing: £6.00
Concessionary Seating: £6.00
Under-16s Standing/Seating: £2.00 if accompanied by a paying adult.

DISABLED INFORMATION

Wheelchairs: Accommodated
Helpers: Please phone the club for information
Prices: Normal prices for the disabled. Free for helpers
Disabled Toilets: Available adjacent to the Main Stand
Contact: (07500) 838068 (Bookings are not necessary)

Travelling Supporters' Information:
Routes: From the North, South and West: Exit the A1 at Blyth services taking the 1st left through to Bawtry. In Bawtry, turn right at the traffic lights onto the A631 straight through to Gainsborough (approx. 11 miles). Go over the bridge to the second set of traffic lights and turn left onto the A159 (Scunthorpe Road). Follow the main road past Tesco on the right through the traffic lights. The ground is situated on right approximately a third of a mile north of the Town Centre; From the East: Take the A631 into Gainsborough and turn right onto the A159. Then as above.

GUISELEY AFC

Founded: 1909
Former Names: None
Nickname: 'The Lions'
Ground: Nethermoor Park, Otley Road, Guiseley, Leeds LS20 8BT
Record Attendance: 3,366 (v Leeds United 26/7/18)
Colours: White shirts with Black shorts
Telephone Nº: 07507 750553
Ground Capacity: 4,021
Seating Capacity: 518
Website: www.guiseleyafc.co.uk
E-mail: admin@guiseleyafc.co.uk

GENERAL INFORMATION

Car Parking: At the ground and in Netherfield Road – Please do not park in Ings Crescent!
Coach Parking: At the ground
Nearest Railway Station: Guiseley (5 minute walk)
Nearest Bus Station: Bus Stop outside the ground
Club Shop: At the ground
Opening Times: Matchdays only
Telephone Nº: 07507 750553

GROUND INFORMATION

Away Supporters' Entrances & Sections:
No usual segregation

ADMISSION INFO (2024/2025 PRICES)

Adult Standing/Seating: £13.00
Concessionary Standing/Seating: £9.00
Ages 11 to 18 Standing/Seating: £5.00
Under-11s Standing/Seating: £1.00 when accompanied by a paying adult

DISABLED INFORMATION

Wheelchairs: 2 spaces are available in the Main Stand
Helpers: Admitted
Prices: Normal prices for disabled fans. Free for helpers
Disabled Toilets: None
Contact: Trudi Miller 07507 750583 (Bookings are advisable) – trudihannaford@guiseleyafc.co.uk

Travelling Supporters' Information:
Routes: Exit the M62 at Junction 28 and take the Leeds Ring Road to the roundabout at the junction of the A65 at Horsforth. Turn left onto the A65 and pass through Rawdon to Guiseley keeping Morrison's supermarket on your left. Pass straight through the traffic lights with the Station pub or your right and the ground is on the right after ¼ mile, adjacent to the cricket field.

HEBBURN TOWN FC

Founded: 1912
Former Names: Reyrolles FC & Hebburn Reyrolles FC
Nickname: 'The Hornets'
Ground: Hebburn Sports Ground, South Drive, Hebburn NE31 1UN
Record Attendance: 1,310 v West Auckland Town
Colours: Black & Yellow shirts and Black shorts
Ground Capacity: 3,000
Seating Capacity: 606
Website: www.hebburntownfc.com
E-mail: info@hebburntownfc.com

GENERAL INFORMATION

Car Parking: Street parking only
Coach Parking: Please contact the club for details.
Nearest Railway Station: Hebburn (5 mins walk)
Club Shop: At the ground
Opening Times: Matchdays only 2.00pm to 6.00pm

GROUND INFORMATION

Away Supporters' Entrances & Sections:
No usual segregation

ADMISSION INFO (2024/2025 PRICES)

Adult Standing/Seating: £10.00
Senior Citizen Standing/Seating: £ 8.00
Under-18s Standing/Seating: £ 2.00
Under-12s Standing/Seating: Free with paying Adult

DISABLED INFORMATION

Wheelchairs: Accommodated
Helpers: Admitted
Prices: Normal prices apply for the disabled but helpers are admitted free of charge.
Disabled Toilets: Available
Contact: None (Bookings are not necessary)

Travelling Supporters' Information:
Routes: From the South: Take the A1(M) to the turn-off for the A194, signposted Tyne Tunnel/South Shields. After approximately 4½ miles, exit at the White Mare Pool Interchange along the B1306 (Mill Lane) then turn right at the T-junction with the A185. The ground is on the left after ½ mile. From the North: Exit the A1(M) onto the A184 (Gateshead Road) and, after approximately 3 miles, turn left along the A185 towards Heworth. The ground is on the left after approximately 1½ miles.

HYDE UNITED FC

Founded: 1885
Former Names: Hyde FC (1885-1917), Hyde United FC (1917-2010), Hyde FC (2010-2015)
Nickname: 'Tigers'
Ground: The Project Solar Stadium, Ewen Fields, Walker Lane, Hyde, Cheshire SK14 5PL
Record Attendance: 7,600 (vs Nelson, 1952)

Colours: Red shirts with Black shorts
Telephone Nº: (0161) 367-7273
Ground Capacity: 4,250
Seating Capacity: 530
Website: www.hydefc.co.uk
E-mail: secretary@hydefc.co.uk

GENERAL INFORMATION

Car Parking: 150 spaces available at the ground
Coach Parking: At the ground
Nearest Railway Station: Newton (¼ mile)
Nearest Bus Station: Hyde
Club Shop: At the ground
Opening Times: Matchdays only
Telephone Nº: (0161) 367-7273

GROUND INFORMATION

Away Supporters' Entrances & Sections:
No usual segregation although it is used as required. When segregation is in operation, Away supporter enter the turnstiles behind the Social Club or in the Walker Stand, as directed.

ADMISSION INFO (2024/2025 PRICES)

Adult Standing: £14.00
Adult Seating: £16.00
Concessionary Standing: £9.00
Concessionary Seating: £11.00
Ages 7 to 17 Standing: £5.00
Ages 7 to 17 Seating: £6.00
Note: Under-7s are admitted free with a paying adult

DISABLED INFORMATION

Wheelchairs: Accommodated in the disabled area
Helpers: Please phone the club for further information
Prices: Please phone the club for further information
Disabled Toilets: Yes
Contact: (0161) 367-7273 (Bookings are not necessary)

Travelling Supporters' Information:
Routes: Exit the M60 at Junction 24 and then exit the M67 at Junction 3 for Hyde. Turn right at the top of the slip road, left at the lights (Morrisons on the left). Turn right at the next set of lights into Lumn Road then turn left at the Give Way sign into Walker Lane. Take the 2nd Car Park entrance near the Leisure Pool and follow the road round for the Stadium.

ILKESTON FC

Founded: 1945 (Re-formed 2010 & 2017)
Former Names: Ilkeston FC
Nickname: 'Robins'
Ground: New Manor Ground, Awsworth Road, Ilkeston, Derbyshire DE7 8JF
Record Attendance: 2,538
Colours: Red shirts with White trim, Red shorts
Telephone Nº: (0115) 930-0386
Ground Capacity: 3,029
Seating Capacity: 550
Website: www.ilkestontownfc.co.uk
E-mail: enquiries@ilkestontownfc.co.uk

GENERAL INFORMATION

Car Parking: At the ground
Coach Parking: At the ground
Nearest Railway Station: Derby (9 miles)
Nearest Bus Station: Ilkeston
Club Shop: At the ground
Opening Times: Matchdays only

GROUND INFORMATION

Away Supporters' Entrances & Sections:
No usual segregation, but can be used if necessary

ADMISSION INFO (2024/2025 PRICES)

Adult Standing: £12.00
Adult Seating: £12.00
Senior Citizen/Under-16s Standing: £8.00
Senior Citizen/Under-16s Seating: £8.00
Note: Under-16s are admitted free of charge when accompanied by a paying adult.

DISABLED INFORMATION

Wheelchairs: Accommodated
Helpers: Admitted
Prices: Please phone the club for further information
Disabled Toilets: Available
Contact: (0115) 930-0386 (Bookings not necessary)

Travelling Supporters' Information:
Routes: Exit the M1 at Junction 26 and take the A610 westwards for 2-3 miles. At the roundabout, turn left to Awsworth then at the next traffic island join the Awsworth Bypass following signs for Ilkeston A6096. After ½ mile turn right into Awsworth Road (signposted Cotmanhay) and the ground is ½ mile on the left.

LANCASTER CITY FC

Founded: 1905
Former Names: Lancaster Athletic FC, Lancaster Town FC and City of Lancaster AFC
Nickname: 'Dolly Blues'
Ground: Giant Axe, West Road, Lancaster LA1 5PE
Record Attendance: 7,500 (1936)

Colours: Blue shirts with White shorts
Telephone Nº: (01524) 382238
Ground Capacity: 3,153
Seating Capacity: 513
Website: www.lancastercityfc.com

GENERAL INFORMATION

Car Parking: At the ground
Coach Parking: At the ground
Nearest Railway Station: Lancaster (2 minutes walk)
Nearest Bus Station: Lancaster (5 minutes walk)
Club Shop: At the ground
Opening Times: Matchdays only
Telephone Nº: None

GROUND INFORMATION

Away Supporters' Entrances & Sections:
No usual segregation

ADMISSION INFO (2024/2025 PRICES)

Adult Standing/Seating: £12.00
Concessionary Standing/Seating: £9.00
Students Standing/Seating: £5.00
Ages 12 to 17 Standing/Seating: £3.00
Note: Under-12s admitted free of charge with a paying adult.

DISABLED INFORMATION

Wheelchairs: Accommodated
Helpers: Admitted
Prices: Normal prices apply
Disabled Toilets: Yes
Contact: (01524) 382238

Travelling Supporters' Information:
Routes: From the South: Exit the M6 at Junction 33 and follow Railway Station signs into the City. Turn left at the traffic lights after Waterstones Bookshop then take the second right passing the Railway Station on the right. Follow the road down the hill and the ground is 1st right; From the North: Exit the M6 at Junction 34 and bear left onto the A683. Go into the one-way system in the City and pass the Police Station. At the next traffic lights by the Revolution pub, follow the road back into the centre, then as from the South, following Railway Station signs.

LEEK TOWN FC

Founded: 1946
Former Names: Abbey Green Rovers FC and Leek Lowe Hamil FC
Nickname: 'The Blues'
Ground: F. Ball Community Stadium, Harrison Park, Macclesfield Road, Leek, Staffordshire ST13 8LD
Record Attendance: 3,512 (1973/74)

Colours: Blue shirts and shorts
Telephone Nº: (01538) 399278
Ground Capacity: 3,600
Seating Capacity: 625
Website: www.pitchero.com/clubs/leektown
E-mail: commercial@leektown.co.uk

GENERAL INFORMATION

Car Parking: 80 spaces available at the ground
Coach Parking: At the ground
Nearest Railway Station: Stoke or Macclesfield (both are 13 miles)
Nearest Bus Station: Leek
Club Shop: At the ground
Opening Times: Matchdays only
Telephone Nº: (01538) 399278
Postal Sales: Yes

GROUND INFORMATION

Away Supporters' Entrances & Sections:
Grace Street entrances for the Grace Street Paddock

ADMISSION INFO (2024/2025 PRICES)

Adult Standing/Seating: £10.00
Child Standing/Seating: £6.00
Note: Under-8s are admitted free with a paying adult

DISABLED INFORMATION

Wheelchairs: 5 spaces available for home fans, 4 for away fans
Helpers: Admitted
Prices: Normal prices apply
Disabled Toilets: Two available
Contact: (01538) 399278 – Derek Goldstraw
(Bookings are not necessary)

Travelling Supporters' Information:
Routes: From the North: Exit the M6 at Junction 19 to Macclesfield then follow the A523 to Buxton Road; From the South: Exit the M6 at Junction 15 to the City Centre then follow A53 Leek Road. The ground is situated ½ mile outside Leek on the Macclesfield side of the A523 Macclesfield to Buxton road.

MACCLESFIELD FC

Founded: 1874 (Re-formed in 2021)
Former Names: Macclesfield Town FC
Nickname: 'The Silkmen'
Ground: Leasing.com Stadium, London Road, Macclesfield, Cheshire SK11 7SP
Record Attendance: 3,502 (2021)

Ground Capacity: 5,500
Seating Capacity: 2,095
Colours: Blue shirts and shorts
Telephone Nº: (01625) 426708
Website: www.macclesfieldfc.com
E-mail: info@macclesfieldfc.com

GENERAL INFORMATION

Car Parking: Ample parking available near the ground
Coach Parking: Near the ground
Nearest Railway Station: Macclesfield (1 mile)
Nearest Bus Station: Macclesfield
Club Shop: At the ground
Opening Times: Weekdays 9.30am to 5.00pm and Saturday matchdays 12.00pm to 3.00pm.
Telephone Nº: (01625) 264686

GROUND INFORMATION

Away Supporters' Entrances & Sections:
John Askey Terrace and the left side of the Moss Lane Stand

ADMISSION INFO (2024/2025 PRICES)

Adult Standing: £17.00
Adult Seating: £17.00
Senior Citizen Standing: £13.00
Senior Citizen Seating: £13.00
Students Standing/Seating: £10.00
Under-18s Standing/Seating: £7.00
Under-12s Standing/Seating: £3.00

FANS WITH DISABILITIES INFORMATION

Wheelchairs: 45 spaces in front of the Estate Road Stand
Helpers: One helper admitted per fan with disabilities
Prices: Normal prices apply for fans with disabilities. Helpers are admitted free of charge
Disabled Toilets: 3 available
Contact: (01625) 426708 (Bookings are necessary)

Travelling Supporters' Information:
Routes: From the North: Exit the M6 at Junction 19 to Knutsford, follow the A537 to Macclesfield. Follow signs for the Town Centre, then for the A523 to Leek. The ground is 1 mile out of the Town Centre on the right; From the South: Exit the M6 at Junction 17 for Sandbach and follow the A534 to Congleton. Then take the A536 to Macclesfield. After passing The Rising Sun on the left, turn right into Moss Lane after approximately ¼ mile . Following this lane will take you to the ground.

MATLOCK TOWN FC

Founded: 1878
Former Names: Hall Leys FC
Nickname: 'The Gladiators'
Ground: The Proctor Cars Stadium, Causeway Lane, Matlock DE4 3AR
Record Attendance: 5,123 (1975)

Colours: Royal Blue shirts and shorts
Ground Capacity: 2,300
Seating Capacity: 560
Website: www.matlocktownfc.co.uk
E-mail: info@matlocktownfc.co.uk

GENERAL INFORMATION

Car Parking: Available in the Town Centre (500 yards)
Coach Parking: Available at the Bus Station (300 yards)
Nearest Railway Station: Matlock (¼ mile)
Nearest Bus Station: Matlock (¼ mile)
Club Shop: At the ground
Opening Times: Weekdays 9.00am – 4.00pm and Saturdays 9.00am to 12.00pm

GROUND INFORMATION

Away Supporters' Entrances & Sections:
No usual segregation

ADMISSION INFO (2024/2025 PRICES)

Adult Standing/Seating: £12.00
Concessionary/Junior Standing/Seating: £8.00
Ages 16 to 18 Standing/Seating: £5.00
Ages 10 to 15 Standing/Seating: £3.00
Note: Under-10s are admitted free with a paying adult

DISABLED INFORMATION

Wheelchairs: Accommodated
Helpers: Admitted
Prices: Normal prices apply
Disabled Toilets: Available
Contact: via E-mail (Bookings are not necessary)

Travelling Supporters' Information:
Routes: Take the A6 to Matlock and at the roundabout by the Bus Station take the A615. The ground is situated on the A615 Matlock to Alfreton road about 500 yards from the Town Centre near Firs Parade.

MATLOCK TOWN FC

Founded: 1878
Former Names: Hall Leys FC
Nickname: 'The Gladiators'
Ground: The Proctor Cars Stadium, Causeway Lane, Matlock DE4 3AR
Record Attendance: 5,123 (1975)
Colours: Royal Blue shirts and shorts
Ground Capacity: 2,300
Seating Capacity: 560
Website: www.matlocktownfc.co.uk
E-mail: info@matlocktownfc.co.uk

GENERAL INFORMATION

Car Parking: Available in the Town Centre (500 yards)
Coach Parking: Available at the Bus Station (300 yards)
Nearest Railway Station: Matlock (¼ mile)
Nearest Bus Station: Matlock (¼ mile)
Club Shop: At the ground
Opening Times: Weekdays 9.00am – 4.00pm and Saturdays 9.00am to 12.00pm

GROUND INFORMATION

Away Supporters' Entrances & Sections:
No usual segregation

ADMISSION INFO (2024/2025 PRICES)

Adult Standing/Seating: £12.00
Concessionary/Junior Standing/Seating: £8.00
Ages 16 to 18 Standing/Seating: £5.00
Ages 10 to 15 Standing/Seating: £3.00
Note: Under-10s are admitted free with a paying adult

DISABLED INFORMATION

Wheelchairs: Accommodated
Helpers: Admitted
Prices: Normal prices apply
Disabled Toilets: Available
Contact: via E-mail (Bookings are not necessary)

Travelling Supporters' Information:
Routes: Take the A6 to Matlock and at the roundabout by the Bus Station take the A615. The ground is situated on the A615 Matlock to Alfreton road about 500 yards from the Town Centre near Firs Parade.

MORPETH TOWN AFC

Founded: 1894
Former Names: Morpeth FC & Morpeth Utd FC
Nickname: The Highwaymen
Ground: Craik Park, Morpeth NE61 2YX
Record Attendance: 1,456 (06/03/2019)

Colours: Amber shirts and Black shorts
Ground Capacity: 2,000
Seating Capacity: 250
Website: www.morpethtownafc.com
E-mail: admin@morpethtownafc.com

GENERAL INFORMATION

Car Parking: At the ground
Coach Parking: At the ground
Nearest Railway Station: Morpeth (1 mile)
Club Shop: At the ground
Opening Times: Matchdays only

GROUND INFORMATION

Away Supporters' Entrances & Sections:
No usual segregation

ADMISSION INFO (2024/2025 PRICES)

Adult Standing/Seating: £12.00
Senior Citizen Standing/Seating: £8.00
Under-16s Standing/Seating: £4.00
Note: Under-5s are admitted free with a paying Adult.

DISABLED INFORMATION

Wheelchairs: Accommodated
Helpers: Admitted
Prices: Normal prices apply for the disabled but helpers are admitted free of charge.
Disabled Toilets: Available
Contact: None (Bookings are not necessary)

Travelling Supporters' Information:
Routes: Exit the A1 at the B1337 (Morpeth) turn-off and, after approximately 1 mile, take the 2nd exit at the roundabout onto the A197. Go straight across at the next roundabout before turning left along the B6524. After approximately ¾ mile turn right into High House Road and the ground is a short way along on the right.

PRESCOT CABLES FC

Founded: 1886
Former Names: Prescot Athletic FC, Prescot Town FC and Prescot FC
Nickname: The Cables
Ground: Joseph Russell Stadium, Eaton Street, Prescot L34 6HB
Record Attendance: 8,122 (1932)
Colours: Amber shirts with Black shorts
Telephone Nº: (0151) 430-0507
Ground Capacity: 2,070
Seating Capacity: 500
Website: www.pitchero.com/clubs/prescotcablesfootballclub
E-mail: Use the contact form on the club's website

GENERAL INFORMATION

Car Parking: At the ground
Coach Parking: At the ground
Nearest Railway Station: Prescot (½ mile)
Nearest Bus Station: Prescot (¼ mile)
Club Shop: At the ground
Opening Times: Matchdays only
Telephone Nº: (0151) 430-0507

GROUND INFORMATION

Away Supporters' Entrances & Sections:
No usual segregation

ADMISSION INFO (2024/2025 PRICES)

Adult Standing: £11.00
Adult Seating: £11.00
Concessionary Standing: £7.00
Concessiony Seating: £7.00
Under-16s Standing: £4.00
Under-16s Seating: £4.00

DISABLED INFORMATION

Wheelchairs: Accommodated
Helpers: Admitted
Prices: Normal prices apply
Disabled Toilets: Available
Contact: (0151) 430-0507 (Bookings are not necessary)

Travelling Supporters' Information:
Routes: Exit the M62 at Junction 7 and take the A57 signposted Rainhill & Prescot. After about 2½ miles, take the 3rd exit at the roundabout. Turn right after ½ mile at the Hope & Anchor pub into Hope Street and the ground is at the end of the road.

STOCKTON TOWN FC

Founded: 1987
Former Names: Hartburn Juniors FC
Nickname: The Anchors
Ground: The Map Group UK Stadium, Bishopton Road West, Stockton-on-Tees TS19 0QD
Record Attendance: 3,300 (2018)

Colours: Yellow shirts and Blue shorts
Telephone Nº: 01642-604915
Ground Capacity: 1,800
Seating Capacity: 250
Website: www.stocktontownfc.com

GENERAL INFORMATION

Car Parking: At the ground
Coach Parking: At the ground
Nearest Railway Station: Thornaby (20 minutes walk)
Club Shop: At the ground
Opening Times: Matchdays only

GROUND INFORMATION

Away Supporters' Entrances & Sections:
No usual segregation

ADMISSION INFO (2024/2025 PRICES)

Adult Standing/Seating: £11.00
Concessionary Standing/Seating: £9.00
Ages 11 to 18 Standing/Seating: £5.00
Under-11s Standing/Seating: £3.00

DISABLED INFORMATION

Wheelchairs: Accommodated
Helpers: Admitted
Prices: Normal prices apply for the disabled but helpers are admitted free of charge.
Disabled Toilets: Available
Contact: None (Bookings are not necessary)

Travelling Supporters' Information:
Routes: Take the A1(M) to the A66(M) and continue on the A66 towards Stockton-on-Tees. Upon entering Stockton, exit the A66 at the A135 (Yarm Road) turn then take the A1027 (signposted Stockton) at the roundabout. Turn left at the 3rd set of traffic lights along Hartburn Lane (signposted Norton) and, after passing a park on the right, move into the right-hand lane. At the next roundabout take the 2nd exit towards Norton then turn left at the 2nd set of traffic lights (near Sainsburys) before turning left for the ground.

WARRINGTON RYLANDS 1906 FC

Founded: 1906
Former Names: Rylands FC & Crossfields/Rylands FC
Nickname: The Blues
Ground: Gorsey Lane, Warrington WA2 7RZ
Record Attendance: 1,809 (vs Warrington Town, 2023)
Colours: Blue shirts and shorts
Ground Capacity: 1,345
Seating Capacity: 250
Website: www.warringtonrylandsfc.co.uk
E-mail: info@warringtonrylandsfc.co.uk

GENERAL INFORMATION

Car Parking: Street parking only
Coach Parking: Please contact the club
Nearest Railway Station: Warrington Central (1½ miles)
Club Shop: At the ground
Opening Times: Matchdays only

GROUND INFORMATION

Away Supporters' Entrances & Sections:
No usual segregation

ADMISSION INFO (2024/2025 PRICES)

Adult Standing: £10.00
Adult Seating: £10.00
Concession Standing: £7.00
Concession Seating: £7.00
Under-16s Standing: £2.00
Under-16s Seating: £2.00

DISABLED INFORMATION

Wheelchairs: Accommodated
Helpers: Admitted
Prices: Normal prices apply for the disabled but helpers are admitted free of charge.
Disabled Toilets: Available
Contact: None (Bookings are not necessary)

Travelling Supporters' Information:
Routes: Exit the M62 at Junction 9 and take the A49 (Winwick Road) into Warrington. Take the A50 (Long Lane) turn-off near Warrington & Vale Royal College and continue along into School Road, then turn right at the traffic lights along Hallfields Road. At the next roundabout, turn left into Norris Street then take the 2nd right along Gorsey Lane. The ground is on the left.

WHITBY TOWN FC

Founded: 1893
Former Names: Whitby United FC
Nickname: 'The Seasiders' or 'The Blues
Ground: The Towbar Express Stadium @ The Turnbull Ground, Upgang Lane, Whitby YO21 3HZ
Record Attendance: 4,500
Colours: Royal Blue shirts and shorts
Ground Capacity: 2,999
Seating Capacity: 622
Website: www.whitbytownfc.com
E-mail: info@whitbytownfc.com

GENERAL INFORMATION

Car Parking: At the ground – passholders only
Coach Parking: At the ground
Nearest Railway Station: Whitby (½ mile)
Nearest Bus Station: Whitby (½ mile)
Club Shop: At the ground
Opening Times: Matchdays only

GROUND INFORMATION

Away Supporters' Entrances & Sections:
No usual segregation but if required at the Upgang Lane end of the ground

ADMISSION INFO (2024/2025 PRICES)

Adult Standing/Seating: £12.00
Concessionary Standing/Seating: £8.00
Ages 17 and 18 Standing/Seating: £4.00
Under-16s Standing/Seating: Free with a paying Adult.

DISABLED INFORMATION

Wheelchairs: Accommodated in a special disabled area
Helpers: Admitted
Prices: Free for the disabled. Helpers charged normal prices
Disabled Toilets: One available
Contact: Via e-mail (Bookings are not necessary)

Travelling Supporters' Information:
Routes: On entering Whitby from the west on either the A169 or A171 road, take the first fork and follow signs for the "West Cliff". Turn left at the Spar shop and garage into Love Lane and continue to the junction with the A174. Turn right onto the A174 and the ground is on the left hand side after approximately 600 yards.

WORKINGTON AFC

Founded: 1884 (Reformed 1921)
Former Names: None
Nickname: 'Reds'
Ground: Borough Park, Workington CA14 2DT
Record Attendance: 21,000 (vs Manchester United)
Colours: Red shirts and shorts
Ground Capacity: 3,100
Seating Capacity: 500
Website: www.workingtonafc.com
E-mail: commercial@workingtonafc.com

GENERAL INFORMATION

Car Parking: Car Park next to the ground
Coach Parking: At the ground
Nearest Railway Station: Workington (¼ mile)
Nearest Bus Station: Workington (½ mile)
Club Shop: At the ground
Opening Times: Matchdays only

GROUND INFORMATION

Away Supporters' Entrances & Sections:
No usual segregation

ADMISSION INFO (2024/2025 PRICES)

Adult Standing/Seating: £13.00
Concessionary Standing/Seating: £9.00
Ages 16 and 17 Standing/Seating: £5.00
Under-16s Standing/Seating: Free upon application for a season card.

DISABLED INFORMATION

Wheelchairs: Accommodated
Helpers: Admitted
Prices: Normal prices apply
Disabled Toilets: Available
Contact: Via e-mail (Bookings are not necessary)

Travelling Supporters' Information:
Routes: Exit the M6 at Junction 40 and take the A66 towards Keswick and Workington. Upon reaching Workington, continue until you reach the traffic lights at the bottom of the hill (with HSBC Bank facing) and turn left towards the town centre. Approach the traffic lights in the middle lane with the Washington Central Hotel on the right and turn right. Continue along this road, crossing a mini-roundabout, a pedestrian crossing and a further set of traffic lights. Upon reaching the railway station, pass through the junction and bear right passing the Derwent Park Rugby League Stadium then bear left and Borough Park is straight ahead.

WORKSOP TOWN FC

Founded: Possibly 1861 (Reformed in 1893)
Former Names: Worksop Town Atletic FC
Nickname: 'The Tigers'
Ground: Windsor Food Service Stadium, Babbage Way, off Sandy Lane, Worksop S80 1UJ
Record Attendance: 2,115

Colours: Amber and Black shirts with Black shorts
Telephone Nº: 07572 769449
Ground Capacity: 2,500
Seating Capacity: 327
Website: www.worksoptownfc.com

GENERAL INFORMATION

Car Parking: Adjacent to the ground
Coach Parking: Adjacent to the ground
Nearest Railway Station: Worksop (2 minutes walk)
Nearest Bus Station: Worksop (2 minutes walk)
Club Shop: At the ground
Opening Times: Matchdays only
Telephone Nº: None

GROUND INFORMATION

Away Supporters' Entrances & Sections:
No usual segregation

ADMISSION INFO (2024/2025 PRICES)

Adult Standing/Seating: £13.00
Concessionary Standing/Seating: £9.00
Ages 12-16 Standing/Seating: £6.00 with a paying Adult
Under 12s Standing/Seating: £3.00 with a paying Adult

DISABLED INFORMATION

Wheelchairs: Accommodated
Helpers: Admitted
Prices: Normal prices apply for the disabled and helpers
Disabled Toilets: Available
Contact: 07572 769449 (Bookings are not necessary)

Travelling Supporters' Information:
Routes: Exit the M1 at Junction 31 from the north or Junction 30 from the South and follow signs for Worksop. After reaching Worksop, carry on to the bypass and, at the 3rd roundabout (next to Sainsburys), turn off following signs for Sandy Lane Industrial Estate. The ground is on the left after half a mile.

The Isthmian League Premier Division

Website www.isthmian.co.uk

Clubs for the 2024/2025 Season

BILLERICAY TOWN FC

Founded: 1880
Former Names: None
Nickname: 'Town' 'Blues'
Ground: The Steel Team Stadium, New Lodge, Blunts Wall Road, Billericay, Essex CM12 9SA
Record Attendance: 4,582 (vs West Ham, 2017)

Colours: Blue shirts and Black shorts
Ground Capacity: 4,800
Seating Capacity: 2,000
Telephone No: (01277) 286474
Website: www.billericaytownfc.co.uk
E-mail: info@billericaytownfc.co.uk

GENERAL INFORMATION

Car Parking: Street parking only
Coach Parking: Please contact the club for information
Nearest Railway Station: Billericay (½ mile)
Club Shop: At the ground
Opening Times: Matchdays only
Telephone No: (01277) 652188

GROUND INFORMATION

Away Supporters' Entrances & Sections:
No usual segregation

ADMISSION INFO (2024/2025 PRICES)

Adult Standing/Seating: £15.00
Concession Standing/Seating: £8.00
Ages 12 to 17 Standing/Seating: £5.00
Under-12s Standing/Seating: £1.00

DISABLED INFORMATION

Wheelchairs: Accommodated
Helpers: Admitted
Prices: Normal prices for disabled fans. Free for helpers
Disabled Toilets: Available in the Clubhouse and the ground
Contact: (01277) 286474 (Bookings are necessary)

Travelling Supporters' Information:
Route: Exit the M25 at Junction 28 and follow the A129 to Billericay. Turn right at the 1st set of traffic lights into Tye Common Road then 2nd right into Blunts Wall Road and the ground is on the right.
Alternative route: Exit the M25 at Junction 29 and take the A129 road from Basildon into Billericay and turn left at the 2nd set of traffic lights into Tye Common Road. Then as above.

BOGNOR REGIS TOWN FC

Founded: 1883
Former Names: None
Nickname: 'The Rocks'
Ground: The MKM Arena, Nyewood Lane, Bognor Regis PO21 2TY
Record Attendance: 3,642 (1984)

Colours: White shirts with Green trim, Green shorts
Ground Capacity: 4,500
Seating Capacity: 367
Website: www.bognorregistownfc.co.uk
E-mail: Via the form on the club's website

GENERAL INFORMATION

Car Parking: Outside the ground at the Sports Club
Coach Parking: None
Nearest Railway Station: Bognor Regis (1 mile)
Nearest Bus Station: Bognor Regis (1 mile)
Club Shop: At the ground
Opening Times: Matchdays only

GROUND INFORMATION

Away Supporters' Entrances & Sections:
No usual segregation

ADMISSION INFO (2024/2025 PRICES)

Adult Standing: £12.00
Adult Seating: £13.00
Concessionary Standing: £12.00
Concessionary Seating: £13.00
Under-18s/Students Standing: £6.00
Under-18s/Students Seating: £7.00

DISABLED INFORMATION

Wheelchairs: Accommodated
Helpers: Admitted
Prices: Normal prices apply for fans with disabilities. Helpers are admitted free of charge
Disabled Toilets: Available
Contact: Via e-mail (Bookings are not necessary)

Travelling Supporters' Information:
Routes: From the West: Take the M27/A27 to Chichester then the A259 and pass through Bersted towards Bognor Regis. Turn right into Hawthorne Road then left into Nyewood Lane – the ground is on the right; From the East: Take the A27 from Brighton/Worthing and turn left onto the A29 at Fontwell Roundabout. Travel along Shripney Road and turn right at the second roundabout towards Bersted on the A259 then left into Hawthorne Road – then as above.

BOWERS & PITSEA FC

Founded: 1946
Former Names: Bowers United FC
Nickname: Bowers
Ground: The Len Salmon Stadium, Crown Avenue, Pitsea SS13 2BE
Record Attendance: 1,800 (vs Billericay Town FC)

Colours: Red & White Striped shirts and Red shorts
Ground Capacity: 2,661
Seating Capacity: 500
Website: www.bowerspitseafc.co.uk
E-mail: bowersfcsecretary@gmail.com

GENERAL INFORMATION

Car Parking: At the ground
Coach Parking: At the ground
Nearest Railway Station: Pitsea (approximately 1 mile)
Club Shop: At the ground
Opening Times: Matchdays only

GROUND INFORMATION

Away Supporters' Entrances & Sections:
No usual segregation

ADMISSION INFO (2024/2025 PRICES)

Adult Standing/Seating: £10.00
Concession Standing/Seating: £7.00
Ages 13 to 17 Standing/Seating: £3.00
Under-13s Standing/Seating: Free with a paying Adult

DISABLED INFORMATION

Wheelchairs: Accommodated
Helpers: Admitted
Prices: Normal prices apply for the disabled but helpers are admitted free of charge.
Disabled Toilets: Available
Contact: Via e-mail (Bookings are not necessary)

Travelling Supporters' Information:
Routes: Exit the M25 at Junction 30 and take the A13 towards Basildon, exiting at the Pitsea turn-off. Take the 1st exit at the roundabout, passing Tesco on the left, then take the 3rd exit at the next roundabout along 'Ashlyns'. Take the 2nd exit at the next roundabout along Rectory Road before turning left into Kenneth Road. Turn right at the T-junction then turn right into Crown Avenue and the ground is on the left.

CANVEY ISLAND FC

Founded: 1926
Former Names: None
Nickname: 'Gulls'
Ground: The Movie Starr Stadium, Park Lane, Canvey Island, Essex SS8 7PX
Record Attendance: 3,553 (15th April 2003)
Colours: Yellow shirts with Sky Blue shorts
Telephone Nº: (01268) 682991
Ground Capacity: 4,100
Seating Capacity: 500
Website: www.canveyislandfc.com
E-mail: info@canveyislandfc.com

GENERAL INFORMATION

Car Parking: 80 spaces available at the ground
Coach Parking: At the ground as required
Nearest Railway Station: South Benfleet (2 miles)
Club Shop: At the ground
Opening Times: Matchdays plus Thursday and Friday evenings
Telephone Nº: (01268) 682991

GROUND INFORMATION

Away Supporters' Entrances & Sections:
Segregation only used when there is a large away support

ADMISSION INFO (2024/2025 PRICES)

Adult Standing: £12.00
Adult Seating: £12.00
Concessionary Standing: £8.00
Concessionary Seating: £8.00
Note: Under-16s are admitted for £3.00 when accompanied by a paying adult

DISABLED INFORMATION

Wheelchairs: Accommodated
Helpers: Admitted
Prices: Concessionary prices apply for the disabled
Disabled Toilets: None
Contact: (01268) 682991(Bookings are recommended)

Travelling Supporters' Information:
Routes: Take the M25 to either the A127 or the A13 (recommended) then follow the A13 towards Basildon and Southend. At the multiple roundabout system, follow signs for Canvey Island on the A130 towards the Town Centre. Keep to the left hand lane through the one-way system for approximately 1½ miles. Continue past the old bus garage and Park Lane is the first turning on the right.

CARSHALTON ATHLETIC FC

Founded: 1905
Former Names: Mill Lane Mission FC & others
Nickname: 'The Robins'
Ground: War Memorial Sports Ground, Colston Avenue, Carshalton SM5 2PW
Record Attendance: 7,800 vs Wimbledon

Colours: Red shirts and shorts
Telephone No: (0208) 6422551
Ground Capacity: 5,000
Seating Capacity: 250
Website: www.carshaltonathletic.co.uk

GENERAL INFORMATION

Car Parking: 80 spaces available at the ground
Coach Parking: At the ground
Nearest Railway Station: Carshalton (200 yards)
Club Shop: At the ground
Opening Times: Matchdays only
Postal Sales: Yes

GROUND INFORMATION

Away Supporters' Entrances & Sections:
No usual segregation

ADMISSION INFO (2024/2025 PRICES)

Adult Standing/Seating: £11.00
Concessionary Standing/Seating: £8.00
Under-18s Standing/Seating: £5.00
Under-5s Standing/Seating: Free with a paying Adult

DISABLED INFORMATION

Wheelchairs: 6 spaces each for home and away fans are available at the end of the Main Stand
Helpers: Admitted
Prices: Free for the disabled. Usual prices for helpers
Disabled Toilets: Available in the Function Hall
Contact: (0208) 6422551 (Bookings are necessary)

Travelling Supporters' Information:
Routes: From London: Pick up the A23 at The Elephant & Castle or the Oval. Continue along the Brixton Road (A23), through Brixton up Brixton Hill and continue past Streatham Hill to Streatham High Road (still on the A23). At the traffic lights on the junction at St. Leonard's Church, cross into Mitcham Lane (A216), continue through Streatham Road and bear left at the traffic lights at Figgs Marsh onto London Road (A217) and follow A217 through Bishopsford Road until reaching the Rose Hill roundabout. At the roundabout, take the 1st exit into Wrythe Lane and continue for 1 mile, then turn right into Colston Avenue just before the railway bridge. The ground is 50 yards on the right. A private road leads to the Stadium and car park; From the M25: Exit at Junction 8 onto the A217 passing Lower Kingswood, Kingswood Burgh Heath and Banstead until the roundabout before the sign to Sutton. Bear left, still on the A217 to the Rose Hill roundabout, take the 4th exit, then as above.

CHATHAM TOWN FC

Founded: 1882
Former Names: None
Nickname: 'The Chats'
Ground: The Bauvill Stadium, Maidstone Road, Bournville Avenue, Chatham ME4 6LR
Record Attendance: 5,000 (1980)
Colours: Red shirts and Black shorts
Telephone Nº: (01634) 401130
Ground Capacity: 3,000
Seating Capacity: 500
Website: www.chathamtownfc.com
E-mail: secretary@chathamtownfc.com

GENERAL INFORMATION

Car Parking: At the ground
Coach Parking: At the ground
Nearest Railway Station: Chatham (½ mile)
Club Shop: At the ground
Opening Times: Matchdays only
Telephone Nº: (01634) 401130

GROUND INFORMATION

Away Supporters' Entrances & Sections:
No segregation

ADMISSION INFO (2024/2025 PRICES)

Adult Standing/Seating: £12.00
Concession Standing/Seating: £8.00
Under-16s Standing/Seating: £3.00

DISABLED INFORMATION

Wheelchairs: Accommodated
Helpers: Admitted
Prices: Normal prices apply for the disabled and helpers
Disabled Toilets: Available
Contact: (01634) 401130 (Bookings are not necessary)

Travelling Supporters' Information:
Routes: Exit the M2 at Junction 3, and follow directions for Chatham & Town Centre, following the A229. Pass Homebase on the left hand side then, at the fork in the road, bear right onto the A230 Maidstone Road. Continue along Maidstone Road, go straight on at the cross roads and you will see a petrol station on the left. Bournville Avenue is opposite the petrol station on the right hand side of the road and, after turning into Bournville Avenue, the entrance to the ground is the first turn on the left.

CHESHUNT FC

Founded: 1946
Former Names: Cheshunt Sports FC
Nickname: 'The Ambers'
Ground: Cheshunt Stadium, Theobalds Lane, Cheshunt EN8 8RU
Record Attendance: 5,000 (vs Bromley – 1950)

Colours: Amber shirts with Black shorts
Telephone Nº: (01992) 625793
Ground Capacity: 3,174
Seating Capacity: 535
Website: www.cheshuntfc.com
E-mail: info@cheshuntfc.com

GENERAL INFORMATION

Car Parking: At the ground
Coach Parking: At the ground
Nearest Railway Station: Theobalds Grove (¼ mile)
Nearest Bus Station: Waltham Cross
Club Shop: None – but some items are available for purchase from the bar at the Social Club

GROUND INFORMATION

Away Supporters' Entrances & Sections:
No usual segregation

ADMISSION INFO (2024/2025 PRICES)

Adult Standing/Seating: £14.00
Concessionary Standing/Seating: £10.00
Ages 13 to 17 Standing/Seating: £6.00
Under-13s Standing/Seating: £2.00

DISABLED INFORMATION

Wheelchairs: Accommodated
Helpers: Admitted
Prices: Normal prices apply
Disabled Toilets: Access to Clubhouse toilets is available
Contact: (01992) 625793 (Bookings are not necessary)

Travelling Supporters' Information:
Routes: Exit the M25 at Junction 25 and take the A1 northwards towards Hertford. Take the 3rd exit at the first roundabout then turn left at the traffic lights and pass under the railway bridge. Take the next turning on the left into Theobalds Lane and the ground is situated on the right after ¼ mile.

CHICHESTER CITY FC

Founded: 2000 (but earlier clubs date back to 1873)
Former Names: Chichester City United FC
Nickname: Lillywhites
Ground: Oaklands Park, Oaklands Way, Chichester, PO19 6AR
Record Attendance: Not known

Colours: Green & White Hooped shirts & Black shorts
Telephone Nº: (01243) 533368
Ground Capacity: 2,000
Seating Capacity: 250
Website: www.chichestercityfc.co.uk

GENERAL INFORMATION

Car Parking: At the ground
Coach Parking: At the ground
Nearest Railway Station: Chichester (1 mile)
Club Shop: At the ground
Opening Times: Matchdays only

GROUND INFORMATION

Away Supporters' Entrances & Sections:
No usual segregation

ADMISSION INFO (2024/2025 PRICES)

Adult Standing/Seating: £10.00
Concessionary Standing/Seating: £5.00
Ages 16 to 18 Standing/Seating: £3.00
Under-17s Standing/Seating: £1.00

DISABLED INFORMATION

Wheelchairs: Accommodated
Helpers: Admitted
Prices: Normal prices apply for the disabled but helpers are admitted free of charge.
Disabled Toilets: Available
Contact: (01243) 533368 (Bookings are not necessary)

Travelling Supporters' Information:
Routes: Take the A27 to the Chichester Bypass and, at the Stockbridge roundabout, exit onto the A286. After approximately ½ mile, bear left onto The Avenue de Chartres and take the 3rd exit at the roundabout. Stay on The Avenue de Chartres for a third of a mile, then take the 2nd exit at the Westgate roundabout onto Orchard Street. After ½ mile, turn right along Churchside to Northgate then left onto Oaklands Way. The ground is on the left.

CRAY VALLEY PAPER MILLS FC

Founded: 1919
Former Names: None
Nickname: The Millers
Ground: The Artic Stadium, Badgers Sports Ground, Middle Park Avenue, Eltham SE9 5HP
Record Attendance: 1,550 (vs Charlton Ath 2023)

Colours: Green shirts and Black shorts
Ground Capacity: 1,550
Seating Capacity: 250
Website: www.crayvalleypmfc.com
E-mail: Via the form on the club's website

GENERAL INFORMATION

Car Parking: At the ground (70 spaces)
Coach Parking: At the ground
Nearest Railway Station: Eltham (20 minute walk)
Club Shop: At the ground
Opening Times: Matchdays only

GROUND INFORMATION

Away Supporters' Entrances & Sections:
No usual segregation

ADMISSION INFO (2024/2025 PRICES)

Adult Standing/Seating: £12.00
Concessionary Standing/Seating: £7.00
Age 11 to 15 Standing/Seating: £5.00
Under-11s Seating: Free with a paying Adult

DISABLED INFORMATION

Wheelchairs: Accommodated
Helpers: Admitted
Prices: Normal prices apply for the disabled but helpers are admitted free of charge.
Disabled Toilets: Available
Contact: Via e-mail (Bookings are not necessary)

Travelling Supporters' Information:
Routes: The stadium is located next to the junction of the A205 (South Circular Road) and the A20 (Sidcup Road). At this junction (Clifton's Roundabout) take the A20, heading south, then take the 1st left along Eltham Palace Road. At the roundabout, take the 1st exit into Middle Park Avenue and the ground is on the left.

CRAY WANDERERS FC

Founded: 1860
Former Names: None
Nickname: 'The Wands'
Ground: Flamingo Park Sports & Leisure, Sidcup Bypass, Chislehurst BR7 6HL
Record Attendance: 840 (vs Cray Valley PM 2024)

Colours: Amber shirts with Black shorts
Ground Capacity: 2,500
Seating Capacity: 299
Website: www.cray-wanderers.com
E-mail: craywanderersfc@gmail.com

GENERAL INFORMATION

Car Parking: at the ground
Coach Parking: At the ground
Nearest Railway Station: New Eltham (1 mile)
Club Shop: At the ground
Opening Times: Matchdays only

GROUND INFORMATION

Away Supporters' Entrances & Sections:
No usual segregation

ADMISSION INFO (2024/2025 PRICES)

Adult Standing/Seating: £12.00
Concessionary Standing/Seating: £6.00

DISABLED INFORMATION

Wheelchairs: Accommodated
Helpers: Admitted
Prices: Normal prices apply for the disabled and helpers
Disabled Toilets: Available
Contact: Via e-mail (Bookings are recommended)

Travelling Supporters' Information:
Routes: The ground is situated right next to the A20 Sidcup Bypass (on the South side of the road) and is accessible directly from the Westbound carriageway heading towards the A205 South Circular Road.

DARTFORD FC

Founded: 1888
Former Names: None
Nickname: 'The Darts'
Ground: Princes Park Stadium, Grassbanks, Darenth Road, Dartford DA1 1RT
Record Attendance: 4,097 (11th November 2006)
Colours: White & Black halved Shirts and Black Shorts
Telephone Nº: (01322) 299991
Ground Capacity: 4,100
Seating Capacity: 642
Website: www.dartfordfc.com
E-mail: reception@dartfordfc.com

GENERAL INFORMATION

Car Parking: At the ground
Coach Parking: At the ground
Nearest Railway Station: Dartford (½ mile)
Nearest Bus Station: Dartford (½ mile) & Bluewater (2 miles)
Club Shop: At the ground plus online sales
Opening Times: Matchdays only – 1.00pm to 6.00pm (the stadium itself is open daily).
Telephone Nº: (01322) 299991

ADMISSION INFO (2024/2025 PRICES)

Adult Standing/Seating: £15.00
Concessionary Standing/Seating: £10.00
Youth (Ages 13 to 16) Standing/Seating: £5.00
Under-12s Standing/Seating: Free with paying Adult

DISABLED INFORMATION

Wheelchairs: 9 spaces available in total around the ground
Helpers: Admitted
Prices: Normal prices for the disabled. Free for helpers
Disabled Toilets: Available behind each goal, in the main reception and on the upper floor.
Contact: (01322) 299991 (Bookings are not necessary)

Travelling Supporters' Information:
Routes: From M25 Clockwise: Exit the M25 at Junction 1B. At the roundabout, take the 3rd exit onto Princes Road (A225) then the second exit at the next roundabout.* Continue downhill to the traffic lights (with the ground on the left), turn left into Darenth Road then take the 2nd left for the Car Park; From M25 Anti-clockwise: Exit the M25 at Junction 2 and follow the A225 to the roundabout. Take the first exit at this roundabout then the 2nd exit at the next roundabout. Then as from * above.

DOVER ATHLETIC FC

Founded: 1983
Former Names: None
Nickname: 'The Whites'
Ground: Crabble Athletic Ground, Lewisham Road, River, Dover CT17 0JB
Record Attendance: 7,000 (vs Folkestone in 1951)

Colours: White shirts and shorts
Telephone Nº: (01304) 822373
Ground Capacity: 5,745
Seating Capacity: 1,500
Website: www.doverathletic.com
E-mail: enquiries@doverathletic.com

GENERAL INFORMATION

Car Parking: Street parking
Coach Parking: Street parking
Nearest Railway Station: Kearsney (1 mile)
Nearest Bus Station: Pencester Road, Dover (1½ miles)
Club Shop: At the ground
Opening Times: Saturdays 9.00am to 12.00pm
Telephone Nº: (01304) 822373

GROUND INFORMATION

Away Supporters' Entrances & Sections:
Segregation only used when required

ADMISSION INFO (2024/2025 PRICES)

Adult Standing/Seating: £15.00
Concessionary Standing/Seating: £14.00
Ages 11 to 17 Standing/Seating: £9.00
Under-12s Standing/Seating: Free with a paying Adult

DISABLED INFORMATION

Wheelchairs: Approximately 6 spaces are available in the Family Stand
Helpers: Admitted
Prices: Normal prices are applied for the disabled, helpers are admitted free of charge.
Disabled Toilets: Three available
Contact: (01304) 822373 (Bookings are not necessary)

Travelling Supporters' Information:
Routes: Take the A2 to the Whitfield roundabout and take the 4th exit. Travel down the hill to the mini-roundabout then turn left and follow the road for 1 mile to the traffic lights on the hill. Turn sharp right and pass under the railway bridge – the ground is on the left after 300 yards.

DULWICH HAMLET FC

Photo courtesy of John Mills @ Altius Photography

Founded: 1893
Former Names: None
Nickname: 'The Hamlet'
Ground: Champion Hill Stadium, Edgar Kail Way, London SE22 8BD
Record Attendance: 3,336 (8th November 2019 vs Carlisle United)

Colours: Navy Blue shirts and shorts with pink trim
Telephone Nº: (0207) 501-9255
Ground Capacity: 3,334
Seating Capacity: 500
Website: www.dulwichhamletfc.co.uk
E-mail: secretary@dulwichhamletfc.co.uk

GENERAL INFORMATION

Car Parking: 50 spaces available at the ground
Coach Parking: At the ground
Nearest Railway Station: East Dulwich (adjacent)
Nearest Tube Station: Brixton (3½ miles)
Club Shop: At the ground
Opening Times: Matchdays only
Telephone Nº: (0207) 501-9255

GROUND INFORMATION

Away Supporters' Entrances & Sections:
No usual segregation

ADMISSION INFO (2024/2025 PRICES)

Adult Standing/Seating: £13.00
Concessionary Standing/Seating: £5.50
Note: Under-13s are admitted free of charge when accompanying a paying adult

DISABLED INFORMATION

Wheelchairs: 10 spaces available in the front of the Main Stand
Helpers: Admitted
Prices: Normal prices apply for fans with disabilities. Helpers are admitted free of charge.
Disabled Toilets: Available behind the disabled area
Contact: (0207) 501-9255 (Bookings are necessary) – or E-mail: commercial@dulwichhamletfc.co.uk

Travelling Supporters' Information:
Routes: From the Elephant & Castle: Go down Walworth Road, through Camberwell's one-way system and along Denmark Hill. Turn left by the railway into Champion Park and then right at the end down Grave Lane to the ground in Dog Kennel Hill; From the South: Come up through Streatham on the A23, turn right to Tulse Hill along the A205 (Christchurch Road) and carry on towards Sydenham. Turn left at The Grove into Lordship Lane and carry on to East Dulwich.

FOLKESTONE INVICTA FC

Founded: 1936
Former Names: None
Nickname: 'The Seasiders'
Ground: The Alkaline Stadium, Cheriton Road, Folkestone, Kent CT19 5JU
Record Attendance: 7,881 (1958)

Colours: Amber & Black striped shirts and Black shorts
Ground Capacity: 4,000
Seating Capacity: 336
Telephone N°: (01303) 221819
Website: www.folkestoneinvictafc.co.uk
E-mail: info@folkestoneinvictafc.co.uk

GENERAL INFORMATION

Car Parking: Street parking
Coach Parking: At the ground
Nearest Railway Station: Folkestone Central and Folkestone West
Club Shop: At the ground
Opening Times: Matchdays only
Telephone N°: (01303) 221819

GROUND INFORMATION

Away Supporters' Entrances & Sections:
No usual segregation

ADMISSION INFO (2024/2025 PRICES)

Adult Standing/Seating: £12.00
Concessionary Standing/Seating: £9.00
Ages 13 to 17 Standing/Seating: £6.00
Note: Under-13s are admitted free of charge when accompanying a paying adult

DISABLED INFORMATION

Wheelchairs: Accommodated
Helpers: Admitted
Prices: Normal prices apply for disabled & helpers
Disabled Toilets: Available in the Clubhouse (ramped access)
Contact: (01303) 221819 (Bookings are not necessary)

Travelling Supporters' Information:
Routes: Exit the M20 at Junction 13, head south on the A20 for ½ mile and at the traffic lights turn left onto the A2034. The ground is about ¼ mile along near the Harvey Grammar School. Parking is available in front of the Stripes Club or the Cricket Ground.

HASHTAG UNITED FC

Founded: 2016
Former Names: None
Nickname: 'The Tags'
Ground: Parkside, Park Lane, Aveley RM15 4PX
Record Attendance: 227 (at Parkside) on 7/9/2024

Colours: Yellow & Blue shirts and Blue shorts
Ground Capacity: 3,500
Seating Capacity: 424
Website: www.hashtagunited.co.uk
E mail: neil@hashtagunited.co.uk

GENERAL INFORMATION

Car Parking: At the ground
Coach Parking: At the ground
Nearest Railway Station: Ockendon (2.9 miles)
Club Shop: At the ground
Opening Times: Matchdays only 2.00pm to 6.00pm

GROUND INFORMATION

Note: The club's contact address is P.O.Box 12343, Brentwood Cm14 9PU

ADMISSION INFO (2024/2025 PRICES)

Adult Standing/Seating: £12.00
Concessionary Standing/Seating: £7.00
Under-12s Standing/Seating: £3.00

DISABLED INFORMATION

Wheelchairs: Accommodated
Helpers: Admitted
Prices: Normal prices apply for the disabled but helpers are admitted free of charge.
Disabled Toilets: Available
Contact: Via e-mail (Bookings are not necessary)

Travelling Supporters' Information:
Routes: Clockwise on the M25, exit at Jct 30/31 and use the 2nd from left lane to the A13 exit for Thurrock (Lakeside) and at Mar Dyke Interchange take 2nd exit then at roundabout exit into Ship Lane. Continue to next roundabout then take 2nd exit onto High Street and continue into Stifford Rd. At roundabout take 1st exit onto Aveley Bypass (B1335) then at roundabout take 3rd exit merging onto Park Lanr and the ground is on the right.

HASTINGS UNITED FC

Founded: 1893
Former Names: Hastings Town FC, Hastings FC and St. Leonard's Amateurs FC
Nickname: 'The U's'
Ground: The Pilot Field, Elphinstone Road, Hastings, TN34 2AX
Record Attendance: 4,888 (1996/97 season)
Colours: Claret & Blue striped shirts & Claret shorts
Telephone Nº: (01424) 444635
Ground Capacity: 4,050
Seating Capacity: 800
Website: www.hastingsunited.com
E-mail: club@hastingsunited.com

GENERAL INFORMATION

Car Parking: Street parking only
Coach Parking: Street parking only
Nearest Railway Station: Hastings (1½ miles)
Club Shop: At the ground
Opening Times: Matchdays only
Telephone Nº: (01424) 444635

GROUND INFORMATION

Away Supporters' Entrances & Sections:
No usual segregation

ADMISSION INFO (2024/2025 PRICES)

Adult Standing/Seating: £13.00
Concessionary Standing/Seating: £9.00
Child Standing/Seating: £3.00

DISABLED INFORMATION

Wheelchairs: 6 spaces available in total
Helpers: Please phone the club for information
Prices: Please phone the club for information
Disabled Toilets: Available in the Social Club
Contact: (01424) 444635 (Bookings are not necessary)

Travelling Supporters' Information:
Routes: From the A21 turn left into St. Helens Road (A2101). After 1 mile turn left into St. Helens Park Road which leads into Downs Road. Follow Downs Road to the end then turn left at the T-junction. The ground is on the right.

HENDON FC

Founded: 1908
Former Names: Christchurch Hampstead FC (1908-1909); Hampstead Town FC (1909-26); Hampstead FC (1926-1933); Golders Green FC (1933-1946)
Nickname: 'Dons' 'Greens'
Ground: Silver Jubilee Park, Townsend Lane, Kingsbury, London NW9 7NE
Record Attendance: 938 (vs Arsenal XI 15/07/2022)

Colours: Green shirts with White shorts
Telephone Nº: (020) 8908-3553
Ground Capacity: 1,900
Seating Capacity: 298
Website: www.hendonfc.net
E-mail: secretaryhendonfc@gmail.com

GENERAL INFORMATION

Car Parking: Street parking
Coach Parking: Contact the club for details
Nearest Railway Station: Hendon
Nearest Tube Station: Kingsbury (20 minute walk)
Club Shop: At the ground
Opening Times: Matchdays only
Telephone Nº: (020) 8908-3553

GROUND INFORMATION

Away Supporters' Entrances & Sections:
No usual segregation

ADMISSION INFO (2024/2025 PRICES)

Adult Standing/Seating: £12.00
Concessionary Standing/Seating: £8.00
Under-18s Standing/Seating: £1.00

DISABLED INFORMATION

Wheelchairs: Accommodated
Helpers: One helper admitted per wheelchair
Prices: Free for each helper with a disabled fan. Extra helpers are charged half normal prices
Disabled Toilets: Please contact the club for details
Contact: (020) 8908-3553 (Bookings are necessary)

Travelling Supporters' Information:
Routes: From Staples Corner travel north along the A5 towards Edgware through West Hendon, passing Sainsbury's on your right, to the junction with Kingsbury Road at the traffic lights. Turn into Kingsbury Road and Townsend Lane is the 3rd turning on the left, at the top of the hill. The ground is in the bottom left-hand corner of the Silver Jubilee Park.

HORSHAM FC

Founded: 1881
Former Names: None
Nickname: 'Hornets'
Ground: The Fusion Aviation Community Stadium, Worthing Road, Horsham RH13 0AD
Record Attendance: 3,000 (14/11/2023)

Colours: Green and Yellow shirts with Green shorts
Telephone Nº: (01403) 458854
Ground Capacity: 3,000
Seating Capacity: 300
Website: www.horshamfc.co.uk
E-mail: admin@horshamfc.co.uk

GENERAL INFORMATION

Car Parking: Limited parking available at the stadium so please use Horsham Park & Ride
Coach Parking: Please contact the club for details
Nearest Railway Station: Horsham (15 minutes walk)
Club Shop: at the ground
Opening Times: Matchdays only

GROUND INFORMATION

Away Supporters' Entrances & Sections:
No usual segregation

ADMISSION INFO (2024/2025 PRICES)

Adult Standing/Seating: £14.00
Concessionary Standing/Seating: £9.00
Under-16s Standing/Seating: £3.00
Under-6s Standing/Seating: Free with a paying Adult

DISABLED INFORMATION

Wheelchairs: Accommodated
Helpers: Admitted
Prices: Normal prices apply for the disabled and helpers
Disabled Toilets: Available
Contact: (01403) 458854 (Bookings are not necessary)

Travelling Supporters' Information:
Routes: The ground is located off the A24 Road to the South of Horsham near the junction with the B2237 (Worthing Road) but as parking is limited, visitors are advised to use Horsham Park & Ride and to ask for the Golf Club for Horsham stop.

LEWES FC

Founded: 1885
Former Names: None
Nickname: 'Rooks'
Ground: The Dripping Pan, Mountfield Road, Lewes BN7 2XD
Record Attendance: 2,500 (vs Newhaven 26/12/47)
Colours: Red & Black striped shirts with White shorts
Telephone Nº: (01273) 470820
Ground Capacity: 3,000
Seating Capacity: 500
Website: www.lewesfc.com
E-mail: info@lewesfc.com

GENERAL INFORMATION

Car Parking: At the ground
Coach Parking: At Lewes Railway Station (adjacent)
Nearest Railway Station: Lewes (adjacent)
Nearest Bus Station: Lewes (½ mile)
Club Shop: At the ground.
Opening Times: Matchdays only

GROUND INFORMATION

Away Supporters' Entrances & Sections:
No usual segregation – otherwise as directed by stewards

ADMISSION INFO (2024/2025 PRICES)

Adult Standing/Seating: £13.00
Concessionary Standing/Seating: £9.00
Junior (Under-16s) Standing/Seating: Free with an Adult

DISABLED INFORMATION

Wheelchairs: Accommodated
Helpers: Admitted
Prices: Normal prices apply for the disabled and helpers
Disabled Toilets: Available
Contact: (01273) 470820

Travelling Supporters' Information:
Routes: From the North: Take the A26 or the A275 to Lewes and follow signs for the Railway Station. Pass the station on the left and take the next left. The ground is adjacent.
From the South and West: Take the A27 to the A26 for the Town Centre. Then as above.

POTTERS BAR TOWN FC

Founded: 1960
Former Names: None
Nickname: 'The Scholars'
Ground: The Lantern Stadium, Parkfield, Watkins Rise, Potters Bar EN6 1DP
Record Attendance: 2,011 (vs Barnet FC 2019)

Colours: Red shirts and White shorts
Telephone Nº: (01707) 654833
Ground Capacity: 2,500
Seating Capacity: 250
Website: www.pitchero.com/clubs/pottersbartownfc

GENERAL INFORMATION
Car Parking: At the ground
Coach Parking: At the ground
Nearest Railway Station: Potters Bar (½ mile)
Nearest Tube Station: High Barnet (4 miles)
Club Shop: None

GROUND INFORMATION
Away Supporters' Entrances & Sections:
No usual segregation

ADMISSION INFO (2024/2025 PRICES)
Adult Standing/Seating: £13.00
Concessionary Standing/Seating: £10.00
Under-16s Standing/Seating: Free with a paying Adult

DISABLED INFORMATION
Wheelchairs: Accommodated
Helpers: Admitted
Prices: Concessionary prices are charged for the disabled and helpers
Disabled Toilets: None
Contact: (01707) 654833 (Bookings are not necessary)

Travelling Supporters' Information:
Routes: Exit the M25 at Junction 24 and take the A111 Southgate Road into Potters Bar.Turn right into the High Street and the ground is situated on the left hand side of the road after 200 yards.

WHITEHAWK FC

Founded: 1945
Former Names: Whitehawk & Manor Farm Old Boys
Nickname: 'The Hawks'
Ground: The Terra Pura Ground, East Brighton Park, Wilson Avenue, Brighton BN2 5TS
Record Attendance: 2,174 (2015/2016 season)

Colours: Red shirts and shorts
Ground Capacity: 3,126
Seating Capacity: 2268
Website: www.whitehawkfc.com
E-mail: johnrosenblatt@whitehawkfc.com

GENERAL INFORMATION

Car Parking: At the ground
Coach Parking: At the ground
Nearest Railway Station: London Road (3¼ miles)
Club Shop: Online sales only

GROUND INFORMATION

Away Supporters' Entrances & Sections:
No usual segregation

ADMISSION INFO (2024/2025 PRICES)

Adult Standing/Seating: £13.00
Concessionary Standing/Seating: £8.00
Ages 13 to 17 Standing/Seating: £5.00
Under-13s Standing/Seating: Free with a paying Adult

DISABLED INFORMATION

Wheelchairs: Accommodated
Helpers: Admitted
Prices: Concessionary prices are charged for the disabled and helpers
Disabled Toilets: None
Contact: Via e-mail (Bookings are not necessary)

Travelling Supporters' Information:
Routes: Take the M23/A23 to the junction with the A27 on the outskirts of Brighton then follow the A27 towards Lewes. After passing Sussex University on the left, take the slip road onto the B2123 (signposted Falmer, Rottingdean) and continue for approximately 2 miles before turning right at the traffic lights into Warren Road by the Downs Hotel. Continue for approximately 1 mile then turn left at the traffic lights into Wilson Avenue. After 1¼ miles, turn left at the foot of the hill into East Brighton Park.

WINGATE & FINCHLEY FC

Founded: 1874 (as Finchley FC)
Former Names: Formed by the amalgamation of Finchley FC and Wingate FC in 1991
Nickname: 'The Blues'
Ground: The Maurice Rebak Stadium, Summers Lane, Finchley, London N12 0PD
Record Attendance: 9,555 (1949/50 season)

Colours: Azure Blue shirts and White shorts
Telephone Nº: (020) 8446-2217
Ground Capacity: 1,500
Seating Capacity: 500
Website: www.wingatefinchley.com
E-mail: secretary@wingatefinchley.com

GENERAL INFORMATION

Car Parking: Street parking only
Coach Parking: At the ground
Nearest Railway Station: New Southgate (2 miles)
Nearest Tube Station: West Finchley (1 mile)
Club Shop: None

GROUND INFORMATION

Away Supporters' Entrances & Sections:
No usual segregation

ADMISSION INFO (2024/2025 PRICES)

Adult Standing/Seating: £12.00
Concessionary Standing/Seating: £8.00
Ages 11 to 18 Standing/Seating: £5.00
Note: Under-11s are admitted free with a paying adult

DISABLED INFORMATION

Wheelchairs: Accommodated
Helpers: Admitted
Prices: Normal prices apply for the disabled and helpers
Disabled Toilets: None
Contact: (020) 8446-2217 (Bookings are not necessary)

Travelling Supporters' Information:
Routes: Exit the A406 North Circular Road at the junction with the A1000 (High Road) and head northwards. After approximately 300 yards, turn right into Summers Lane and the Stadium is on the right hand side of the road just after the Fitness Centre.

THE SOUTHERN FOOTBALL LEAGUE PREMIER DIVISION CENTRAL

Address

Messenger House, 35 St. Michael's Square,
Gloucester GL1 1HX

Website www.southern-football-league.co.uk

Clubs for the 2024/2025 Season

AFC SUDBURY

Founded: 1999
Former Names: Formed by the amalgamation of Sudbury Town FC and Sudbury Wanderers FC in 1999
Nickname: 'Yellows'
Ground: The MEL Group Stadium, Brundon Lane, Sudbury CO10 7HN
Record Attendance: 2,000 (vs Colchester Utd 2021)
Colours: Yellow shirts with Blue shorts
Telephone Nº: (01787) 736856
Ground Capacity: 2,500
Seating Capacity: 250
Website: www.afcsudbury.co.uk
E-mail: secretary@afcsudbury.co.uk

GENERAL INFORMATION

Car Parking: At the ground
Coach Parking: At the ground
Nearest Railway Station: Sudbury (1½ miles)
Club Shop: At the ground
Opening Times: Matchdays only
Telephone Nº: (01787) 736856

GROUND INFORMATION

Away Supporters' Entrances & Sections:
No usual segregation

ADMISSION INFO (2024/2025 PRICES)

Adult Standing/Seating: £12.00
Concessionary Standing/Seating: £9.00
Note: Under-16s are admitted free of charge when accompanied by a paying adult

DISABLED INFORMATION

Wheelchairs: Accommodated
Helpers: Admitted
Prices: Normal prices apply for the disabled and helpers
Disabled Toilets: Available
Contact: (01787) 736856 (Bookings are not necessary)

Travelling Supporters' Information:
Routes: From the South: Take the A131 to Sudbury. On descending the hill into Sudbury, turn left at first set of traffic lights (by the Kings Head), and then take the first right into Brundon Lane. The road narrows before reaching ground on the right hand side; From the North: Enter Sudbury and follow signs for Halstead/Chelmsford. Cross the river bridge and pass under the old rail bridge, then turn right at the traffic lights (Kings Head) into Bulmer Road and the first right again into Brundon Lane.
Sat Nav: Use postcode CO10 7HN

AFC TELFORD UNITED

Founded: 2004
Former Names: Formed after Telford United FC went out of business. TUFC were previously known as Wellington Town FC
Nickname: 'The Bucks'
Ground: The SEAH Stadium, The Bucks Way, Wellington, Telford TF1 2TU
Record Attendance: 4,215 (vs Kendal Town 2005)
Colours: White shirts with Black shorts
Telephone Nº: (07572) 236037
Ground Capacity: 6,380
Seating Capacity: 2,000
Website: www.telfordunited.com
E-mail: enquiries@afctu.co.uk

GENERAL INFORMATION

Car Parking: At the ground (£4.00 charge for cars)
Coach Parking: At the ground
Nearest Railway Station: Wellington
Nearest Bus Station: Wellington
Club Shop: At the ground
Opening Times: Saturday matchdays only from 1.30pm.
Telephone Nº: (07572) 236037

GROUND INFORMATION

Away Supporters' Entrances & Sections:
No usual segregation

ADMISSION INFO (2024/2025 PRICES)

Adult Standing/Seating: £13.00
Concessionary Standing/Seating: £10.00
Ages 17 and 18 Standing/Seating: £6.00
Under-17s Standing/Seating: £3.00
Under-12s Standing/Seating: £1.00 with a paying adult

DISABLED INFORMATION

Wheelchairs: Accommodated at both ends of the ground
Helpers: Admitted
Prices: Concessionary prices apply for disabled supporters. Helpers are admitted free of charge
Disabled Toilets: Available
Contact: (07572) 236037 (Bookings are not necessary)

Travelling Supporters' Information:
Routes: Exit the M54 at Junction 6 and take the A518. Go straight on at the first roundabout, take the second exit at the next roundabout then turn left at the following roundabout. Follow the road round to the right then turn left into the car park.

ALVECHURCH FC

Founded: 1929
Former Names: None
Nickname: The Church
Ground: Lye Meadow, 53 Redditch Road, Alvechurch B48 7RS
Record Attendance: 13,500 (in 1965)

Colours: Yellow shirts and Black shorts
Telephone Nº: (0121) 445-2929
Ground Capacity: 3,000
Seating Capacity: 250
Website: www.alvechurchfc.club

GENERAL INFORMATION

Car Parking: At the ground (£2.00 charge)
Coach Parking: please contact club
Nearest Railway Station: Alvechurch (20 minute walk)
Club Shop: At the ground
Opening Times: Matchdays only 2.00pm to 6.00pm

GROUND INFORMATION

Away Supporters' Entrances & Sections:
No usual segregation

ADMISSION INFO (2024/2025 PRICES)

Adult Standing/Seating: £12.00
Concessionary Standing/Seating: £10.00
Under-18s Standing/Seating: £7.00
Under-13s Standing/Seating: Free with a paying adult

DISABLED INFORMATION

Wheelchairs: Accommodated
Helpers: Admitted
Prices: Normal prices apply for the disabled but helpers are admitted free of charge.
Disabled Toilets: Available
Contact: (0121) 445-2929 (Bookings are not necessary)

Travelling Supporters' Information:
Routes: Exit the M42 at junction 2 and take the A441 towards Redditch. At the end of the dual carriageway take the 2nd exit onto the B4120 signposted for Alvechurch and the ground is approximately 1 mile along on the right side of the road.

BANBURY UNITED FC

Founded: 1931
Former Names: Spencer Villa FC and Banbury Spencer FC
Nickname: 'The Puritans'
Ground: The Banbury Plant Hire Community Stadium, Station Approach, Banbury OX16 5AB
Record Attendance: 7,160 (vs Oxford City – 1948)

Colours: Red and Gold shirts with Red shorts
Ground Capacity: 6,500
Seating Capacity: 250
Website: www.banburyunitedfc.co.uk
E-mail: info@banburyunitedfc.co.uk

GENERAL INFORMATION

Car Parking: At the ground (up to 200 spaces)
Coach Parking: At the ground
Nearest Railway Station: Banbury (adjacent)
Nearest Bus Station: Banbury
Club Shop: At the ground
Opening Times: Matchdays only

GROUND INFORMATION

Away Supporters' Entrances & Sections:
No usual segregation

ADMISSION INFO (2024/2025 PRICES)

Adult Standing/Seating: £14.00
Concessionary Standing/Seating: £10.00
Under-18s Standing/Seating: £5.00
Student Standing/Seating: £8.00
Under-11s Standing/Seating: Free with a paying adult

DISABLED INFORMATION

Wheelchairs: 6 spaces available in total
Helpers: Admitted
Prices: Normal prices apply
Disabled Toilets: Available
Contact: Via e-#mail (see above)

Travelling Supporters' Information:
Routes: Exit the M40 at Junction 11 and head towards Banbury. Go straight on at the first roundabout then left at the next into Concorde Avenue. Continue straight on at the next roundabout then turn left at the traffic lights. Take the 1st turning on the right into Station Approach then take the single track road on the extreme right of the Station which leads to the Stadium.

BARWELL FC

Founded: 1992
Former Names: Formed by the amalgamation of Barwell Athletic FC and Hinckley FC in 1992
Nickname: 'The Canaries'
Ground: Kirkby Road Sports Ground, Kirkby Road, Barwell LE9 8FQ
Record Attendance: 1,279

Colours: Yellow and Green shirts with Green shorts
Telephone Nº: (01455) 843067
Ground Capacity: 2,500
Seating Capacity: 256
Website: www.pitchero.com/clubs/barwell

GENERAL INFORMATION

Car Parking: At the ground
Coach Parking: At the ground
Nearest Railway Station: Hinckley (3¾ miles)
Club Shop: None

GROUND INFORMATION

Away Supporters' Entrances & Sections:
No usual segregation

ADMISSION INFO (2024/2025 PRICES)

Adult Standing/Seating: £12.00
Concessionary Standing/Seating: £8.00
Under-16s Standing/Seating: £4.00
Under-11s Standing/Seating: Free with a paying Adult

DISABLED INFORMATION

Wheelchairs: Accommodated
Helpers: Admitted
Prices: Normal prices apply for the disabled and helpers
Disabled Toilets: Available
Contact: (01455) 843067 (Bookings are not necessary)

Travelling Supporters' Information:
Routes: Exit the M69 at Junction 1 and take the A5 (Watling Street) towards Nuneaton. At the 3rd roundabout, take the 2nd exit onto the A47 (Dodwells Road) and follow to Barwell, crossing the A447. After crossing the A447, turn left at the roundabout and head into Barwell along The Common and follow into Chapel Street. Go straight on at the roundabout then turn immediately right along Kirkby Road. After approximately ¼ mile, the entrance to the ground is on the right, opposite the cemetery. The football ground itself is behind the cricket field.

BEDFORD TOWN FC

Founded: 1908 (Re-formed in 1989)
Former Names: None
Nickname: 'Eagles'
Ground: The Eyrie Stadium, Meadow Lane, Cardington, Bedford MK44 3LW
Record Attendance: 3,000 (6th August 1993)

Colours: Shirts are Blue with White trim, Blue shorts
Telephone Nº: (01234) 831558
Ground Capacity: 3,000
Seating Capacity: 300
Website: www.pitchero.com/clubs/bedfordtownfootballclub
E-mail: Via the form on the club's website

GENERAL INFORMATION

Car Parking: At the ground
Coach Parking: At the ground
Nearest Railway Station: Bedford Midland (3 miles)
Nearest Bus Station: Greyfriars, Bedford (3 miles)
Club Shop: At the ground
Opening Times: Matchdays only
Telephone Nº: (01234) 831558

GROUND INFORMATION

Away Supporters' Entrances & Sections:
No usual segregation

ADMISSION INFO (2024/2025 PRICES)

Adult Standing/Seating: £14.00
Concessionary Standing/Seating: £10.00
Under-16s Standing/Seating: £8.00
Note: Under-10s are admitted free with a paying adult.

DISABLED INFORMATION

Wheelchairs: Accommodated
Helpers: Admitted
Prices: Normal prices apply
Disabled Toilets: Available
Contact: (01234) 831558 (Bookings are not necessary)

Travelling Supporters' Information:
Routes: From the M1: Exit the M1 at Junction 13 onto the A421. Follow this the the bypass at the Sandy exit and take the A603 towards Sandy. The ground is on the left just before the lay-by; From the A1: Take the Sandy exit, go through Willington and the ground is on the right; From Bedford: Follow signs for Sandy and take Cardington Road out of town. The ground is on the left past 2 mini-roundabouts.

BIGGLESWADE TOWN FC

Founded: 1874
Former Names: Biggleswade FC
Nickname: 'The Waders'
Ground: Langford Road, Biggleswade SG18 9JT
Record Attendance: Approximately 2,000
Colours: Green & White striped shirts, Green shorts
Ground Capacity: 3,000
Seating Capacity: 300
Website: www.pitchero.com/clubs/biggleswadetownfc
E-mail: Via the form on the club's website

GENERAL INFORMATION

Car Parking: At the ground
Coach Parking: At the ground
Nearest Railway Station: Biggleswade (½ mile)
Club Shop: At the ground
Opening Times: Matchdays only

GROUND INFORMATION

Away Supporters' Entrances & Sections:
No usual segregation

ADMISSION INFO (2024/2025 PRICES)

Adult Standing/Seating: £10.00
Concessionary Standing/Seating: £8.00
Note: Under-16s are admitted free of charge when accompanied by a paying adult

DISABLED INFORMATION

Wheelchairs: Accommodated
Helpers: Admitted
Prices: Normal prices apply for the disabled and helpers
Disabled Toilets: Available
Contact: Via e-mail (Bookings are not necessary)

Travelling Supporters' Information:
Routes: The Stadium is located just to the South of the A1 at Biggleswade. Exit the A1 at the northernmost roundabout by the Sainsbury's superstore and follow the A6001 (Hill Lane) into Biggleswade. Continue heading southwards along the A6001 into Shortmead Street then turn right at the mini-roundabout into St. Andrews Street. Continue along then turn right at the traffic lights shortly after the bend in the road onto Hitchin Street. Go straight on at the next two roundabouts, pass under the A1 and the entrance to the ground is on the right, after approximately 200 yards.

BISHOP'S STORTFORD FC

Founded: 1874
Former Names: None
Nickname: 'Blues' 'Bishops'
Ground: The RDA Stadium, Woodside Park, Dunmow Road, Bishop's Stortford CM23 5RG
Record Attendance: 3,555 (2000)

Colours: Blue shirts and White shorts
Telephone Nº: (01279) 306456
Ground Capacity: 4,525
Seating Capacity: 525
Website: www.bsfc.co.uk
E-mail: info@bsfc.co.uk

GENERAL INFORMATION

Car Parking: 150 spaces at the ground (£2.00 fee)
Coach Parking: At the ground (bookings required)
Nearest Railway Station: Bishop's Stortford (25 minute walk)
Club Shop: At the ground
Opening Times: Matchdays only 1.30pm to 5.00pm
Telephone Nº: (01279) 306456

GROUND INFORMATION

Away Supporters' Entrances & Sections:
No usual segregation

ADMISSION INFO (2024/2025 PRICES)

Adult Standing/Seating: £15.00
Concessionary Standing/Seating: £10.00
Student Standing/Seating: £8.00
Under-16s Standing/Seating: £1.00
Note: Under-12s are admitted free of charge when accompanied by a paying adult.

DISABLED INFORMATION

Wheelchairs: Accommodated in the disabled section
Helpers: Admitted
Prices: Free of charge for the disabled and helpers
Disabled Toilets: Yes
Contact: (01279) 306456 (Bookings are not necessary)

Travelling Supporters' Information:
Routes: Exit the M11 at junction 8 and take the A1250 towards Bishop Stortford. Turn left at the first roundabout and the ground is first right opposite the Golf Club (the entrance is between Industrial Units).

BROMSGROVE SPORTING FC

Founded: 2009
Former Names: None
Nickname: 'The Rouslers'
Ground: The UK Electrical Stadium, Victoria Ground, Birmingham Road, Bromsgrove B61 0DR
Record Attendance: 3,349 (vs Cleethorpes Town 11th March 2017)

Colours: Green & White striped shirts, Green shorts
Telephone Nº: (07454) 451655
Ground Capacity: 4,893
Seating Capacity: 394
Website: www.bromsgrovesporting.co.uk

GENERAL INFORMATION

Car Parking: 200 spaces available at the ground
Coach Parking: By Police Direction
Nearest Railway Station: Bromsgrove (1½ miles)
Nearest Bus Station: 500 yards
Club Shop: At the ground
Opening Times: Weekdays 9.00am to 1.00pm and also at all home matches
Telephone Nº: (01527) 876949

GROUND INFORMATION

Away Supporters' Entrances & Sections:
No usual segregation

ADMISSION INFO (2024/2025 PRICES)

Adult Standing/Seating: £12.00
Concessionary Standing/Seating: £9.00
Ages 12 to 17 Standing/Seating: £3.00
Ages 3 to 11 Standing/Seating: £1.00 with a paying adult

DISABLED INFORMATION

Wheelchairs: 6 spaces are available (more if necessary) outside of the Police Control Room
Prices: £10.00 for disabled but helpers are free
Disabled Toilets: Available
Contact: (07454) 451655 (Bookings are necessary)

Travelling Supporters' Information:
Routes: From the North: Exit the M42 at Junction 1 and follow the A38 towards Bromsgrove. Upon entering Bromsgrove, follow the signs for the Town Centre at the traffic lights. Victoria Ground is approximately 2 minutes drive down the road opposite Lidl on the right hand side; From the South: Exit the M5 at Junction 4 onto the A38. Then as above.

HALESOWEN TOWN FC

Founded: 1873
Former Names: None
Nickname: 'The Yeltz'
Ground: The Grove, Old Hawne Lane, Halesowen, West Midlands B63 3TB
Record Attendance: 5,000 (19th November 1955)
Colours: Shirts are Blue with White trim, White shorts
Ground Capacity: 3,150
Seating Capacity: 525
Website: www.ht-fc.co.uk
E-mail: secretary@halesowentown.com

GENERAL INFORMATION

Car Parking: 20 spaces available at the Social Club.
Coach Parking: Available near to the ground
Nearest Railway Station: Old Hill (2 miles)
Nearest Bus Station: Halesowen Town Centre
Club Shop: At the ground
Opening Times: Matchdays only

GROUND INFORMATION

Away Supporters' Entrances & Sections:
No usual segregation

ADMISSION INFO (2024/2025 PRICES)

Adult Standing/Seating: £12.00
Concessionary Standing/Seating: £9.00
Ages 13 to 17 Standing/Seating: £5.00
Under-13s Standing/Seating: £2.00 when accompanied by a paying adult.

DISABLED INFORMATION

Wheelchairs: 5 spaces available in total situated at the side of the Main Seating Stand
Helpers: Admitted
Prices: Free of charge for the disabled
Disabled Toilets: Available near the Main Stand
Contact: Via e-mail (Bookings are not necessary)

Travelling Supporters' Information:
Routes: Exit the M5 at Junction 3 and follow the A456 towards Kidderminster. At the first roundabout, turn right onto the A458 towards Dudley. Turn left at the next roundabout and follow signposts onto the A458 towards Stourbridge. Take the 3rd exit at the next roundabout and the ground is on the left hand side after approximately 400 yards.

HARBOROUGH TOWN FC

Founded: 1975
Former Names: Harborough Town Juniors FC which merged with Spencer United FC in 2008
Nickname: The Bees
Ground: Harborough Town Community Football Ground, Northampton Road, Market Harborough, LE16 9HF

Record Attendance: 1,022 (15th January 2022)
Colours: Yellow shirts and shorts
Telephone Nº: (01858) 469352
Ground Capacity: 2,400
Seating Capacity: 250
Website: www.harboroughtownfc.org
E-mail: Via the form on the club's website

GENERAL INFORMATION

Car Parking: At the ground
Coach Parking: At the ground
Nearest Railway Station: Market Harborough (1 mile)
Club Shop: At the ground
Opening Times: Saturdays only 9.00 to 12.00

GROUND INFORMATION

Away Supporters' Entrances & Sections:
No usual segregation

ADMISSION INFO (2024/2025 PRICES)

Adult Standing/Seating: £12.00
Concession Standing/Seating: £8.00
Under-16s Standing/Seating: £3.00

DISABLED INFORMATION

Wheelchairs: Accommodated
Helpers: Admitted
Prices: Normal prices apply for the disabled but helpers are admitted free of charge.
Disabled Toilets: Available
Contact: (01858) 469352 (Bookings are not necessary)

Travelling Supporters' Information:
Routes: From the South: Exit the A14 at junction 2 and head north on the A508 for approximately 8 miles passing through Great Oxendon. Go past the Market Harborough Golf Club on the right and take the 1st exit at the roundabout. The ground is then a short way along on the right; From the North: Take the A6 southbound, exit at the A4304 turn-off follow into Market Harborough. After passing the Railway Station on the right, turn left into Kettering Road then take the 3rd exit at the roundabout into Springfield Street before bearing left along Northampton Road on the A508. After passing the Leisure Centre on the right and Protheroe's Garage on the left, turn right at the roundabout for the ground.

HITCHIN TOWN FC

Founded: 1865 (Re-formed in 1928)
Former Names: Hitchin FC
Nickname: 'The Canaries'
Ground: Top Field, Fishponds Road, Hitchin, Hertfordshire SG5 1NU
Record Attendance: 7,878 (1955)
Colours: Yellow & Green shirts with Green shorts
Ground Capacity: 3,529
Seating Capacity: 409
Telephone Nº: (01462) 459028 (Matchdays only)
Website: www.hitchintownfc.co.uk
E-mail: Via the form on the club's website

GENERAL INFORMATION

Car Parking: Space for 200 cars at the ground
Coach Parking: At the ground
Nearest Railway Station: Hitchin (1 mile)
Club Shop: At the ground
Opening Times: Matchdays only

GROUND INFORMATION

Away Supporters' Entrances & Sections:
No usual segregation

ADMISSION INFO (2024/2025 PRICES)

Adult Standing/Seating: £15.00
Concessionary Standing/Seating: £11.00
Ages 13 to 19 Standing/Seating: £5.00
Under-13s Standing/Seating: £3.00 with a paying adult

DISABLED INFORMATION

Wheelchairs: 10 spaces are available by the Main Stand
Helpers: Admitted
Prices: Normal prices apply
Disabled Toilets: Available at rear of the Main Stand
Contact: 07803 202498 (Please book in advance)

Travelling Supporters' Information:
Routes: Take A1(M) to Junction 8 and follow A602 signposted to Hitchin. At Three Moorhens roundabout, take 3rd exit onto A600 towards Bedford. At next roundabout go straight over onto one-way system, go straight over at traffic lights, turn right at next roundabout and the turnstiles are immediately on the left. The Car Park turning is 50 yards further on; Alternatively, take M1 to Junction 10 and follow well appointed signs to Hitchin via A505. On approach to Hitchin go straight over initial mini-roundabout, turn left at next roundabout and turnstiles are situated immediately on the left; By Train: From Hitchin Station turn right outside station approach and follow the road around the DIY store into Nightingale Road which leads past the Woolpack Pub to The Victoria. Take Bunyan Road at The Victoria which leads into Fishponds Road.

KETTERING TOWN FC

Founded: 1872
Former Names: Kettering FC
Nickname: 'The Poppies'
Ground: Latimer Park, Polwell Lane, Burton Latimer, Kettering NN15 5PS
Record Attendance: 11,526 (at Rockingham Road)

Colours: Red and Black striped shirts & Black shorts
Telephone Nº: (01536) 217006
Ground Capacity: 3,029
Seating Capacity: 606
Website: www.ketteringtownfc.com
E-mail: info@ketteringtownfc.com

GENERAL INFORMATION

Car Parking: At the ground
Coach Parking: At the ground
Nearest Railway Station: Kettering (3 miles)
Nearest Bus Station: Kettering
Club Shop: None

GROUND INFORMATION

Away Supporters' Entrances & Sections:
Station Road end when segregation is in force

ADMISSION INFO (2024/2025 PRICES)

Adult Standing/Seating: £15.00
Concessionary Standing/Seating: £10.00
Under-16s Standing/Seating: £2.00

DISABLED INFORMATION

Wheelchairs: Accommodated around the ground
Helpers: Admitted
Prices: Normal prices apply for the disabled fans with registered carers admitted free of charge
Disabled Toilets: Available around the ground
Contact: (01536) 217006

Travelling Supporters' Information:
Routes: The ground is located on the A6 about 350 yards north of the junction with the A45 (over the bridge). This is approximately 6 miles south of the A14.

LEISTON FC

Founded: 1880
Former Names: Leiston Works Athletic FC
Nickname: 'The Blues'
Ground: The Watson & Hillhouse Stadium, Victory Road, Leiston IP16 4DQ
Record Attendance: 1,250 (2008/2009 season)
Colours: Blue & White striped shirts & Blue shorts
Telephone Nº: (01728) 830308
Ground Capacity: 2,250
Seating Capacity: 250
Website: www.leistonfc.co.uk
E-mail: Via the form on the club's website

GENERAL INFORMATION

Car Parking: At the ground
Coach Parking: At the ground
Nearest Railway Station: Saxmundham (3½ miles)
Nearest Tube Station: Saxmundham
Club Shop: At the ground
Opening Times: Matchdays or by appointment only
Telephone Nº: (01728) 830308

GROUND INFORMATION

Away Supporters' Entrances & Sections:
No usual segregation

ADMISSION INFO (2024/2025 PRICES)

Adult Standing/Seating: £12.00
Concessionary Standing/Seating: £9.00
Student Standing/Seating: £7.00
Ages 5 to 16 Standing/Seating: £3.00
Under-5s: Admitted free of charge with a paying adult

DISABLED INFORMATION

Wheelchairs: Accommodated
Helpers: Admitted
Prices: Normal prices apply for the disabled and helpers
Disabled Toilets: Available in the Clubhouse
Contact: (01728) 830308 (Bookings are necessary)

Travelling Supporters' Information:
Routes: Leiston is located midway between Lowestoft and Ipswich, about 3½ miles due east of Saxmundham. Take the A12 to Saxmundham then the B1119 road to Leiston. Upon reaching Leiston, continue along the B1119 (Waterloo Avenue) to the junction with the B1069 and turn right along Park Hill. Take the first turning on the left into Victory Road and the ground is located on the right-hand side by the junction with Huntingfield Road.

LOWESTOFT TOWN FC

Founded: 1880
Former Names: East Suffolk FC and Lowestoft FC
Nickname: 'The Trawler Boys'
Ground: Crown Meadow, Love Road, Lowestoft, NR32 2PA
Record Attendance: 5,000 (1967)
Colours: Blue shirts and shorts
Telephone Nº: (01502) 573818
Ground Capacity: 3,000
Seating Capacity: 466
Website: www.lowestofttownfc.co.uk

GENERAL INFORMATION

Car Parking: Street parking only
Coach Parking: At Lowestoft College
Nearest Railway Station: Lowestoft (½ mile)
Club Shop: At the ground
Opening Times: Matchdays only 11.00am to 5.00pm
Telephone Nº: (01502) 567280

GROUND INFORMATION

Away Supporters' Entrances & Sections:
No usual segregation

ADMISSION INFO (2024/2025 PRICES)

Adult Standing/Seating: £12.00
Concessionary Standing/Seating: £9.00
Under-16s Standing/Seating: £2.00

DISABLED INFORMATION

Wheelchairs: Accommodated
Helpers: Admitted
Prices: Concessionary prices apply for both the disabled and helpers
Disabled Toilets: Available
Contact: (01502) 573818 (Bookings are necessary)

Travelling Supporters' Information:
Routes: Take the A146 or the A12 to Lowestoft Town Centre then head north on the A12 Katwijk Way Road. Turn left into Love Road for the ground.

REDDITCH UNITED FC

Founded: 1891
Former Names: Redditch Town FC
Nickname: 'The Reds'
Ground: The Valley Stadium, Bromsgrove Road, Redditch B97 4AU
Record Attendance: 5,500 (vs Bromsgrove 1954/55)
Colours: Red shirts, shorts and socks
Telephone Nº: (01527) 67450
Ground Capacity: 3,500
Seating Capacity: 516
Website: www.redditchunited.co.uk
E-mail: info@redditchunited.co.uk

GENERAL INFORMATION

Car Parking: At the ground
Coach Parking: At the ground
Nearest Railway Station: Redditch (¼ mile)
Nearest Bus Station: Redditch (¼ mile)
Club Shop: At the ground
Opening Times: Matchdays only

GROUND INFORMATION

Away Supporters' Entrances & Sections:
No segregation

ADMISSION INFO (2024/2025 PRICES)

Adult Standing/Seating: £11.00
Concessionary Standing/Seating: £8.00
Under-16s Standing: £1.00
Under-16s Seating: £2.00

DISABLED INFORMATION

Wheelchairs: Accommodated
Helpers: Admitted
Prices: Normal prices apply to both helpers and disabled
Disabled Toilets: Available
Contact: (01527) 67450 (Bookings are not necessary)

Travelling Supporters' Information:
Routes: Exit the M42 at Junction 2 and follow the A441 towards Redditch. Upon reaching the outskirts of Reddith, take the 4th exit at the roundabout (signposted Batchley) then turn left at the traffic lights into Birmingham Road. Take the next right into Clive Road then left into Hewell Road. Continue to the T-junction and turn right, passing the Railway Station on the right. Continue through the traffic lights and entrance to the ground is situated on the right hand side after about ¼ mile.

ROYSTON TOWN FC

Founded: 1875
Former Names: None
Nickname: The Crows
Ground: Garden Walk, Royston SG8 7HP
Record Attendance: 1,152 (2019-2020 season)

Colours: White shirts and Black shorts
Telephone Nº: (01763) 241204
Ground Capacity: 5,000
Seating Capacity: 300
Website: www.roystontownfc.co.uk
E-mail: secretary@roystontownfc.co.uk

GENERAL INFORMATION

Car Parking: Use Main Town Hall Car Park (3 minutes walk)
Coach Parking: Please contact the club
Nearest Railway Station: Royston (1 mile)
Club Shop: At the ground
Opening Times: Matchdays only

GROUND INFORMATION

Away Supporters' Entrances & Sections:
No usual segregation

ADMISSION INFO (2024/2025 PRICES)

Adult Standing/Seating: £12.00
Concessionary Standing/Seating: £8.00
Under-16s Standing/Seating: £4.00

DISABLED INFORMATION

Wheelchairs: Accommodated
Helpers: Admitted
Prices: Normal prices apply for the disabled but helpers are admitted free of charge.
Disabled Toilets: Available
Contact: (01763) 241204 (Bookings are not necessary)

Travelling Supporters' Information:
Routes: Exit the M11 at junction 11 and take the A10 to Royston. On the outskirts of the town, take the 2nd exit at the roundabout and continue for about ½mile. After passing St Mary's School on the right, take the next left into Garden Walk for the ground.

SPALDING UNITED FC

Founded: 1905
Former Names: Fulney Institute FC and Victoria FC
Nickname: 'The Tulips'
Ground: Sir Halley Stewart Field, Winfrey Avenue, Spalding PE11 1DA
Record Attendance: 6,972 (1982)
Colours: Royal Blue shirts and shorts
Telephone Nº: (07586) 584515
Ground Capacity: 2,700
Seating Capacity: 300
Website: www.spaldingunited.net
E-mail: secretary@spaldingunited.net

GENERAL INFORMATION

Car Parking: A car park is just outside the ground
Coach Parking: Outside the ground
Nearest Railway Station: Spalding (adjacent)
Club Shop: At the ground
Opening Times: Matchdays only
Telephone Nº: (07586) 584515

GROUND INFORMATION

Away Supporters' Entrances & Sections:
No usual segregation

ADMISSION INFO (2024/2025 PRICES)

Adult Standing/Seating: £12.00
Concessionary Standing/Seating: £7.00
Under-18s Standing/Seating: £4.00
Under-11s Standing/Seating: Free with an adult

DISABLED INFORMATION

Wheelchairs: Accommodated
Helpers: Admitted
Prices: Reduced prices apply for the disabled and helpers
Disabled Toilets: Available
Contact: (07586) 584515 (Bookings are not necessary)

Travelling Supporters' Information:
Routes: Spalding is situated just to the west of the A16 Stamford to Boston road. Take the A16 to Spalding then join the A151 Holbeach Road at the roundabout and follow into Spalding Town Centre, crossing over the River Welland into West Elloe Avenue then left into Pinchbeck Road. Turn right into King's Road then left into Winfrey Avenue. The ground is then on the left.

STAMFORD AFC

Founded: 1896
Former Names: None
Nickname: The Daniels or the Dannies
Ground: The Zeeco Stadium, Borderville Sports Centre, Ryhall Road, Stamford PE9 1US
Record Attendance: 1,572 (10th July 2019)
Colours: Red shirts and shorts
Telephone Nº: (01780) 751471
Ground Capacity: 2,000
Seating Capacity: 300
Website: www.pitchero.com/clubs/stamfordafc
E-mail: Via the form on the club's website

GENERAL INFORMATION

Car Parking: At the ground
Coach Parking: Please contact the club
Nearest Railway Station: Stamford (1½ miles)
Club Shop: At the ground
Opening Times: Matchdays only
Telephone Nº: (01780) 751471

GROUND INFORMATION

Away Supporters' Entrances & Sections:
No usual segregation

ADMISSION INFO (2024/2025 PRICES)

Adult Standing/Seating: £12.00
Concession Standing/Seating: £8.00
Ages 12 to 17 Standing/Seating: £4.00
Under-12s Standing/Seating: Free with a paying adult

DISABLED INFORMATION

Wheelchairs: Available within the Centre
Helpers: Admitted
Prices: Normal prices apply
Disabled Toilets: Available
Contact: (01780) 751471

Travelling Supporters' Information:
Routes: From the North: Exit the A1 at the B1081 turn-off (signposted for Stamford) continue into Great Casterton. Turn left along Ryhall Road and after about 2½ miles, turn right at the T-junction onto the B1176 then right again onto the A6121. The ground is situated on the right after approximately 1½ miles; From the South: Exit the A1 at the A606 turn-off (signposted for Oakham), then take the 1st right along Water Lane passing over the A1. At the junction with the B1081 in Great Casterton continue across into Ryhall Road then follow the directions as above from the North.

ST. IVES TOWN FC

Founded: 1887
Former Names: None
Nickname: The Saints
Ground: Quattro-Tech Stadium, Westwood Road, St. Ives PE27 6DT
Record Attendance: 1,523 (2nd May 2016)

Colours: Black & White striped shirts and Black shorts
Ground Capacity: 2,000
Seating Capacity: 250
Website: www.stivestownfc.co.uk
E-mail: Via the form on the club's website

GENERAL INFORMATION

Car Parking: Burgess Hall (opposite ground)
Coach Parking: Please contact the club
Nearest Railway Station: Huntingdon (6½miles)
Club Shop: At the ground
Opening Times: Matchdays only

GROUND INFORMATION

Away Supporters' Entrances & Sections:
No usual segregation

ADMISSION INFO (2024/2025 PRICES)

Adult Standing/Seating: £11.00
Concession Standing/Seating: £8.00
Students/Military Personnel: £5.00
Ages 12 to 15 Standing/Seating: £2.00
Under-12s Standing/Seating: Free with a paying adult

DISABLED INFORMATION

Wheelchairs: Accommodated
Helpers: Admitted
Prices: Normal prices apply for the disabled but helpers are admitted free of charge.
Disabled Toilets: Available
Contact: Via e-mail (Bookings are not necessary)

Travelling Supporters' Information:
Routes: Exit the A14 at junction 24 (the Swavesey exit), then take the A1307 (Huntingdon Road) to the junction with the A1096. Turn North along Harrison Way and continue to the roundabout with the A1123 Needingworth Road. Take the 1st exit and continue along Needingworth Road at the next roundabout then along St. Audrey Lane before taking the slip road into Ramsey Road. The ground is Westwood Road on the right, opposite the Fire Station.

STOURBRIDGE FC

Founded: 1876
Former Names: Stourbridge Standard FC
Nickname: 'The Glassboys'
Ground: War Memorial Athletic Ground, High Street, Amblecote, Stourbridge DY8 4HN
Record Attendance: 5,726 (1974)
Colours: Red and White striped shirts with Red shorts
Telephone Nº: (01384) 394040
Ground Capacity: 2,626
Seating Capacity: 250
Website: www.stourbridgefc.com
E-mail: admin@stourbridgefc.com

GENERAL INFORMATION

Car Parking: At the ground
Coach Parking: Please contact the club for information
Nearest Railway Station: Stourbridge Town (¾ mile)
Club Shop: At the ground
Opening Times: Matchdays only from 1 hour before kick-off
Telephone Nº: (01384) 394040

GROUND INFORMATION

Away Supporters' Entrances & Sections:
No usual segregation

ADMISSION INFO (2024/2025 PRICES)

Adult Standing/Seating: £13.00
Concessionary Standing/Seating: £10.00
Ages 13 to 17 Standing/Seating: £7.00
Ages 6 to 12 Standing/Seating: £5.00

DISABLED INFORMATION

Wheelchairs: Accommodated
Helpers: Admitted
Prices: Normal prices apply for the disabled and helpers
Disabled Toilets: Available
Contact: (01384) 394040 (Bookings are necessary)

Travelling Supporters' Information:
Routes: From the South: Exit the M5 at Junction 4 and take the A491 to Stourbridge. Continue along the A491, pass Hagley then go through Pedmore and Old Swinford before joining the Stourbridge Ring Road (one-way). Follow the lane signs for Wolverhampton A491. Pass through three sets of traffic lights before reaching the ground which is on the left hand side of the road, opposite the Royal Oak Public House; From the North or East: Exit the M5 at Junction 3 and take the A456 towards Stourbridge and Kidderminster. After about five miles, turn right at the traffic lights in Hagley to join the A491 and follow into Stourbridge passing through Pedmore and Old Swinford onto the Stourbridge Ring-Road (one-way) as above.

STRATFORD TOWN FC

Founded: 1941
Former Names: Stratford Rangers FC
Nickname: The Bards
Ground: The Arden Garages Stadium, Knights Lane, Tiddington, Stratford-upon-Avon CV37 7BZ
Record Attendance: 2,800 (7th November 2021)
Colours: Orange & Blue shirts and Blue shorts
Ground Capacity: 3,000
Seating Capacity: 250
Website: www.stratfordtownfc.co.uk
E-mail: Via the form on the club's website

GENERAL INFORMATION

Car Parking: At the ground
Coach Parking: Please contact the club
Nearest Railway Station: Stratford-upon-Avon (1½miles)
Club Shop: At the ground
Opening Times: Matchdays only

GROUND INFORMATION

Away Supporters' Entrances & Sections:
No usual segregation

ADMISSION INFO (2024/2025 PRICES)

Adult Standing/Seating: £12.00
Concessionary Standing/Seating: £8.00
Under-18s Standing/Seating: £5.00
Under-12s Standing/Seating: Free with a paying adult

DISABLED INFORMATION

Wheelchairs: Accommodated
Helpers: Admitted
Prices: Normal prices apply for the disabled but helpers are admitted free of charge.
Disabled Toilets: Available
Contact: Via e-mail (Bookings are not necessary)

Travelling Supporters' Information:
Routes: Exit the M40 at junction 15 and take the A46 towards Stratford. At the 1st roundabout, turn left onto the A439 and keep to the left-hand lane through the one-way system before turning left onto the B4086 Tiddington Road towards Wellesbourne. Continue for approximately 1 mile and, after passing the NFU Mutual Building on the right, take the next left into Knights Lane. The ground is on the right, shortly after the school.

The Southern Football League Premier Division South

Address

Messenger House, 35 St. Michael's Square,
Gloucester GL1 1HX

Website www.southern-football-league.co.uk

Clubs for the 2024/2025 Season

AFC TOTTON

Founded: 1886
Former Names: Totton FC
Nickname: 'The Stags'
Ground: The Snows Stadium, Salisbury Road, Totton, Southampton SO40 2RW
Record Attendance: 2,061 (6th May 2024)

Colours: Blue shirts and shorts
Telephone Nº: (023) 8086-8981
Ground Capacity: 3,000
Seating Capacity: 500
Website: www.afctotton.com
E-mail: enquiries@afctotton.com

GENERAL INFORMATION

Car Parking: At the Industrial Park adjacent to the ground
Coach Parking: At the ground
Nearest Railway Station: Totton (1½ miles)
Club Shop: At the ground
Opening Times: Matchdays only

GROUND INFORMATION

Away Supporters' Entrances & Sections:
No usual segregation

ADMISSION INFO (2024/2025 PRICES)

Adult Standing/Seating: £14.00
Concessionary Standing/Seating: £10.00
Ages 13 to 17 Standing/Seating: £10.00
Under-13s Standing/Seating: £7.00

DISABLED INFORMATION

Wheelchairs: Accommodated
Helpers: Admitted
Prices: £10.00 for the disabled and helpers free
Disabled Toilets: Available
Contact: (023) 8086-8981 (Bookings are not necessary)

Travelling Supporters' Information:
Routes: Exit the M27 at Junction 2 and head south on the A326. Almost immediately, take the slip road and turn left to join the A36 heading into Totton. The ground is located on the left hand side of the road after approximately ¾ mile, just before the roundabout for Calmore Industrial Park. Spectators travelling by car should turn left at this roundabout and can use the car park of Mansell Construction Services Ltd. which is immediately on the right after entering the Industrial Park.

BASINGSTOKE TOWN FC

Founded: 1896
Former Names: None
Nickname: 'Dragons'
Ground: Winklebury Football Complex, Winklebury Way, Basingstoke RG23 8BF
Record Attendance: 1,577 (vs South Park 2023)
Colours: Yellow and Blue shirts with Blue shorts
Ground Capacity: 2,000
Seating Capacity: 250
Website: www.btfc.co.uk
E-mail: club@btfc.co.uk

GENERAL INFORMATION

Car Parking: Please park at Loddon Vale Bowling Club (SatNav RG22 6PG), which is a 5 minute walk away.
Coach Parking: Please contact the club
Nearest Railway Station: Basingstoke (1.5 miles)
Club Shop: Online sales only

GROUND INFORMATION

Away Supporters' Entrances & Sections:
No usual segregation

ADMISSION INFO (2024/2025 PRICES)

Adult Standing/Seating: £12.50
Concessionary Standing/Seating: £8.50
Under-18s Standing/Seating: £5.50
Under-12s Standing/Seating: £2.50

DISABLED INFORMATION

Wheelchairs: spaces are available
Helpers: Admitted
Prices: Normal prices for the disabled. Free for helpers
Disabled Toilets: Available
Contact: Via e-mail (Bookings are not necessary)

Travelling Supporters' Information:
Routes: Exit the M3 at Junction 6 and take the A339 into Basingstoke. Continue along the Ringway North after the Oakridge village turn-off to the Winklebury roundabout then turn left along the Ringway West. The complex is a short distance along on the right.

BRACKNELL TOWN FC

Founded: 1896
Former Names: Old Bracknell Wanderers FC and Bracknell FC
Nickname: The Robins
Ground: The SB Stadium, Bottom Meadow, Sandhurst Memorial Park, Yorktown Road, Sandhurst GU47 9BJ
Record Attendance: 1,950 (vs Ipswich Town 7/11/22)
Colours: Red shirts and White shorts
Telephone N°: (01344) 412305
Ground Capacity: 2,500
Seating Capacity: 250
Website: www.bracknelltownfc.com
E-mail: operations@bracknelltownfc.com

GENERAL INFORMATION

Car Parking: Pyes Acre Car Park (SatNav GU47 9AH)
Coach Parking: Please contact the club
Nearest Railway Station: Blackwater (1¾ miles)
Club Shop: At the ground
Opening Times: Matchdays only

GROUND INFORMATION

Away Supporters' Entrances & Sections:
No usual segregation

ADMISSION INFO (2024/2025 PRICES)

Adult Standing/Seating: £13.00
Concessionary Standing/Seating: £9.00
Under-18s Standing/Seating: £1.00

DISABLED INFORMATION

Wheelchairs: Accommodated
Helpers: Admitted
Prices: Normal prices apply for the disabled but helpers are admitted free of charge.
Disabled Toilets: Available
Contact: (01344) 412305 (Bookings are not necessary)

Travelling Supporters' Information:
Routes: Exit the M3 at junction 4 and take the A331 Northwards to the A30 at Blackwater. Continue along the A3095 (Marshall Road) and turn left down the A321 (Yorktown Road). The stadium is on the left after a short distance.

CHERTSEY TOWN FC

Founded: 1890
Former Names: None
Nickname: 'The Curfews'
Ground: Alwyns Lane, Chertsey KT16 9DW
Record Attendance: 2,150 (4th December 1993)

Colours: Blue & White striped shirts with White shorts
Telephone Nº: (01932) 561744
Ground Capacity: 2,500
Seating Capacity: 250
Website: www.chertseytownfc.co.uk
E-mail: info@chertseytownfc.co.uk

GENERAL INFORMATION

Car Parking: Limited number of spaces at the ground
Coach Parking: At the ground
Nearest Railway Station: Chertsey (½ mile)
Nearest Bus Station: Chertsey
Club Shop: None, but a limited selection of CTFC items are available at the ground on matchdays.

GROUND INFORMATION

Away Supporters' Entrances & Sections:
No usual segregation

ADMISSION INFO (2024/2025 PRICES)

Adult Standing/Seating: £12.00
Concessionary Standing/Seating: £8.00
Under-18s Standing/Seating: £3.00

DISABLED INFORMATION

Wheelchairs: Accommodated
Helpers: Admitted
Prices: £8.00 for the disabled. Helpers are admitted free
Disabled Toilets: Available in the clubhouse
Contact: (01932) 561744 (Bookings are not necessary)

Travelling Supporters' Information:
Routes: Exit the M25 at Junction 11 and take the A317 (St. Peter's Way) towards Chertsey. Take the first exit at the roundabout into Chertsey Road then continue straight on into Fordwater Road (B387) which then becomes Weir Road. At the T-junction at the bottom of Weir Road, turn left into Bridge Road (B375), continue along as the road sweeps left then bears left into London Street. Take the second exit at the mini-roundabout (with the shopping centre on the left) and continue into Windsor Street, turning left into Alwyns Lane shortly after the road bends right. The ground is on the left, a short way along Alwyns Lane.

DORCHESTER TOWN FC

Founded: 1880
Former Names: None
Nickname: 'The Magpies'
Ground: The Avenue Stadium, Weymouth Avenue, Dorchester, Dorset DT1 2RY
Record Attendance: 4,159 (1st January 1999)
Colours: Black & White striped shirts with Black shorts
Telephone Nº: (01305) 267623
Ground Capacity: 5,229
Seating Capacity: 710
Website: www.dorchestertownfc.co.uk
E-mail: office@dorchestertownfc.co.uk

GENERAL INFORMATION

Car Parking: 350 spaces available at the ground (£1.00 fee)
Coach Parking: At the ground
Nearest Railway Station: Dorchester South and West (both 1 mile)
Nearest Bus Station: Nearby
Club Shop: At the ground
Opening Times: During 1st team matchdays only
Telephone Nº: (01305) 267623

GROUND INFORMATION

Away Supporters' Entrances & Sections:
Main Stand side when segregated (not usual)

ADMISSION INFO (2024/2025 PRICES)

Adult Standing/Seating: £14.00
Concessionary Standing/Seating: £11.00
Ages 12 to 16 Standing/Seating: £6.00
Under-12s Standing/Seating: £3.00

DISABLED INFORMATION

Wheelchairs: 10 spaces available each for home and away fans at the North West End of the terracing
Helpers: Admitted
Prices: Normal prices apply
Disabled Toilets: 2 available near the disabled area
Contact: (01305) 267623 (Bookings are not necessary)

Travelling Supporters' Information:
Routes: Take the Dorchester Bypass (A35) from all directions. The ground is on the South side of town, adjacent to a roundabout at the intersection with the A354 to Weymouth. Alternatively, take Weymouth signs from Dorchester Town Centre for 1½ miles.

FROME TOWN FC

Founded: 1904
Former Names: None
Nickname: 'The Robins' or 'The Dodge'
Ground: Badgers Hill, Berkley Road, Frome, BA11 2EH
Record Attendance: 8,000 (1954)

Colours: Red shirts and shorts
Ground Capacity: 3,000
Seating Capacity: 500
Website: www.wearebа11.com
E-mail: secretary@frometownafc.co.uk

GENERAL INFORMATION

Car Parking: At the ground
Coach Parking: At the ground
Nearest Railway Station: Frome (1 mile)
Club Shop: At the ground
Opening Times: Matchdays only

GROUND INFORMATION

Away Supporters' Entrances & Sections:
No usual segregation

ADMISSION INFO (2024/2025 PRICES)

Adult Standing/Seating: £12.00
Concessionary Standing/Seating: £9.00
Student Standing/Seating: £4.00
Under-16s Standing/Seating: £2.00

DISABLED INFORMATION

Wheelchairs: Accommodated
Helpers: Admitted
Prices: Normal prices apply for the disabled and helpers
Disabled Toilets: None
Contact: Via e-mail (Bookings are necessary)

Travelling Supporters' Information:
Routes: Take the A36 southwards from Bath and, after passing Beckington, join the A361 heading towards Frome. At the next roundabout, join the B3090 and continue into Frome from the north. Turn left into Berkley Road shortly after passing the Cricket Ground on the left and Aldersmith Stadium is on the right hand side after a short distance.

GLOUCESTER CITY FC

Founded: 1883
Former Names: Gloucester YMCA
Nickname: 'The Tigers'
Ground: Tigerturf Stadium, Sudmeadow Road, Hempsted, Gloucester GL2 5HD
Record Attendance: 8,326 (1956)

Colours: Yellow & Red Banded shirts with Red shorts
Telephone Nº: None
Ground Capacity: 4,000
Seating Capacity: 700
Website: www.gloucestercityafc.com
E-mail: secretary@gcafc.co.uk

GENERAL INFORMATION

Car Parking: Available at the ground for disabled fans only. However, free parking is available in Sainsbury's car park which is a 5 minute walk from St. Ann Way (SatNav GL2 5SA)
Nearest Railway Station: Gloucester (1 mile)
Nearest Bus Station: Gloucester
Club Shop: At the ground
Opening Times: Matchdays only

GROUND INFORMATION

Away Supporters' Entrances & Sections:
No usual segregation

ADMISSION INFO (2024/2025 PRICES)

Adult Standing/Seating: £14.00 (On the day)
Cocessions Standing/Seating: £11.00 (On the day)
Ages 12 to 17 Standing/Seating: £6.00 (On the day)
Under-12s: Admitted free of charge with a paying adult
Note: Ticket prices are £2.00 cheaper if pre-booked.

DISABLED INFORMATION

Wheelchairs: Accommodated
Helpers: Admitted
Prices: Normal prices apply for disabled fans
Disabled Toilets: Available
Contact: secretary@gtafc.co.uk (Bookings are necessary)

Travelling Supporters' Information:
Routes: Take the A40 into the City Centre towards the Historic Docks, then take Severn Road and turn right into Hempstead Lane. Take the second right into Sudmeadow Road and the ground is 50 yards on the left.

GOSPORT BOROUGH FC

Founded: 1944
Former Names: Gosport Borough Athletic FC
Nickname: 'The Boro'
Ground: Privett Park, Privett Road, Gosport, PO12 3SX
Record Attendance: 4,770 (1951)

Colours: Yellow & Blue shirts with Blue shorts
Telephone Nº: (023) 9252-5797 (Matchdays only)
Fax Number: (01329) 235961
Ground Capacity: 4,500
Seating Capacity: 1,000
Website: www.gosportboroughfc.com

GENERAL INFORMATION

Car Parking: At the ground
Coach Parking: At the ground
Nearest Railway Station: Fareham (5½ miles)
Club Shop: At the ground
Opening Times: Matchdays only

GROUND INFORMATION

Away Supporters' Entrances & Sections:
No usual segregation

ADMISSION INFO (2024/2025 PRICES)

Adult Standing/Seating: £13.00
Concessionary Standing/Seating: £9.00
Under-18s Standing/Seating: £5.00
Note: Under-12s are admitted free of charge when accompanied by a paying adult

DISABLED INFORMATION

Wheelchairs: Accommodated
Helpers: Admitted
Prices: Normal prices apply for the disabled and helpers
Disabled Toilets: Available
Contact: (023) 9252-5797 (Bookings are not necessary)

Travelling Supporters' Information:
Routes: Exit the M27 at Junction 11 and follow take the A27 Eastern Way towards Gosport. Turn left at the roundabout to join the A32 Gosport Road and head south into Gosport. Continue along the A32 as it becomes Fareham Road then, at the second roundabout in a junction with two roundabouts, take the 3rd exit (signposted Alverstoke, Stokes Bay, Privett Park) into Military Road. Continue straight down this road, pass the playing fields on the left, then turn left at the roundabout into Privett Road. The entrance to the ground is the 4th turning on the left, just after the junction with Privett Place.

HANWELL TOWN FC

Founded: 1920
Former Names: None
Nickname: The London Geordies
Ground: The Powerday Stadium, Reynolds Field, Perivale UB6 8TL
Record Attendance: 624 (vs Brentford XI 2023)

Colours: Black & White striped shirts & Black shorts
Telephone Nº: (0208) 998-1701
Ground Capacity: 3,000
Seating Capacity: 250
Website: www.hanwelltown.com
E-mail: club@hanwelltown.com

GENERAL INFORMATION

Car Parking: At the ground
Coach Parking: Please contact the club
Nearest Railway Station: South Greenford (1½ miles)
Club Shop: At the ground
Opening Times: Matchdays only

GROUND INFORMATION

Away Supporters' Entrances & Sections:
No usual segregation

ADMISSION INFO (2024/2025 PRICES)

Adult Standing/Seating: £13.00
Concessionary Standing/Seating: £7.00
Under-18s Standing/Seating: £5.00

DISABLED INFORMATION

Wheelchairs: Accommodated
Helpers: Admitted
Prices: Normal prices apply for the disabled but helpers are admitted free of charge.
Disabled Toilets: Available
Contact: (0208) 998-1701 (Bookings are not necessary)

Travelling Supporters' Information:
Routes: The Stadium is located adjacent to the A40 (Western Avenue) at the B456 Perivale (Argyle Road) turn-off.

HAVANT & WATERLOOVILLE FC

Founded: 1998
Former Names: Formed by the amalgamation of Waterlooville FC and Havant Town FC
Nickname: 'The Hawks'
Ground: Westleigh Park, Martin Road, Havant, PO9 5TH
Record Attendance: 4,400 (2006/07)
Colours: White shirts and shorts
Telephone Nº: (023) 9278-7822 (Ground)
Ground Capacity: 5,300
Seating Capacity: 710
Website: www.havantandwaterloovillefc.co.uk
E-mail: generalmanager@havantandwaterloovillefc.co.uk

GENERAL INFORMATION

Car Parking: Space for 300 cars at the ground
Coach Parking: At the ground
Nearest Railway Station: Havant (1 mile)
Nearest Bus Station: Town Centre (1½ miles)
Club Shop: At the ground
Opening Times: Matchdays only
Telephone Nº: 07768 271143

GROUND INFORMATION

Away Supporters' Entrances & Sections:
No usual segregation

ADMISSION INFO (2024/2025 PRICES)

Adult Standing/Seating: £15.00
Concessionary Standing/Seating: £10.00
Student Standing/Seating: £10.00
Note: When accompanied by a paying adult, children under the age of 16 are admitted free of charge.

DISABLED INFORMATION

Wheelchairs: 12 spaces available in the Main Stand
Helpers: Admitted
Prices: Normal prices for disabled fans. Free for helpers
Disabled Toilets: Two available
Contact: (023) 9226-7822 (Bookings are necessary)

Travelling Supporters' Information:
Routes: From London or the North take the A27 from Chichester and exit at the B2149 turn-off for Havant. Take the 2nd exit off the dual carriageway into Bartons Road and then the 1st right into Martin Road for the ground; From the West: Take the M27 then the A27 to the Petersfield exit. Then as above.

HUNGERFORD TOWN FC

Founded: 1886
Former Names: Hungerford Swifts FC
Nickname: 'The Crusaders'
Ground: Town Ground, Bulpit Lane, Hungerford, RG17 0AY
Record Attendance: 1,684 (vs Sudbury Town)
Colours: White shirts with Black shorts
Ground Capacity: 2,500
Seating Capacity: 276
Website: www.hungerfordtown.com
E-mail: Via the form on the club's website

GENERAL INFORMATION

Car Parking: At the ground and at the local school
Coach Parking: At the ground
Nearest Railway Station: Hungerford (½ mile)
Club Shop: At the ground
Opening Times: Matchdays only

GROUND INFORMATION

Away Supporters' Entrances & Sections:
No usual segregation

ADMISSION INFO (2024/2025 PRICES)

Adult Standing/Seating: £12.00
Concessionary Standing/Seating: £9.00
Ages 11 to 17 Standing/Seating: £4.00
Note: Under-11s are admitted free of charge when accompanied by a paying adult.

DISABLED INFORMATION

Wheelchairs: Accommodated
Helpers: Admitted free of charge
Prices: Concessionary prices for the disabled.
Disabled Toilets: Available
Contact: Via e-mail (Bookings are not necessary)

Travelling Supporters' Information:
Routes: Exit the M4 at Junction 14 and take the A338 towards Hungerford. Upon reaching Hungerford, turn right at the roundabout onto the A4 Bath Road, turn left at the next rounabout into Charnham Street then turn left again into Bridge Street (A338). The road becomes the High Street and pass under the railway line, carry straight on over three mini-roundabouts then take the next left into Priory Road. Continue to the end of the street and continue left into Priory Road then take the 3rd turning on the left into Bulpit Lane. The entrance to the ground is on the left shortly after crossing the junction with Priory Avenue.

MARLOW FC

Founded: 1870
Former Names: Great Marlow FC
Nickname: 'The Blues'
Ground: Alfred Davies Memorial Ground,
Oak Tree Road, Marlow SL7 3ED
Record Attendance: 3,000 (1994)

Colours: Royal Blue shirts and shorts
Ground Capacity: 3,000
Seating Capacity: 250
Website: www.marlowfc.co.uk
E-mail: info@marlowfc.co.uk

GENERAL INFORMATION

Car Parking: At the ground
Coach Parking: At the ground
Nearest Railway Station: Marlow (¾ mile)
Club Shop: Online sales only

GROUND INFORMATION

Away Supporters' Entrances & Sections:
No usual segregation

ADMISSION INFO (2024/2025 PRICES)

Adult Standing/Seating: £12.00
Concessionary Standing/Seating: £8.00
Ages 13 to 18 Standing/Seating: £2.00
Ages 6 to 12 Standing/Seating: £1.00
Under-6s Standing/Seating: Free with a paying adult

DISABLED INFORMATION

Wheelchairs: Accommodated
Helpers: Admitted
Prices: Normal prices apply for the disabled. Helpers are admitted free of charge
Disabled Toilets: None
Contact: Via e-mail (Bookings are recommended)

Travelling Supporters' Information:
Routes: Exit the M40 at Junction 4 and take the A404 towards Marlow. Take the first exit for the A4155, follow the A4155 towards Marlow and turn right immediately after the Esso service station called 'On The Run' into Maple Rise. Cross directly over the crossroads into Oak Tree Road and the ground can be found approximately on the left after approximately 100 yards.

MERTHYR TOWN FC

Founded: 1908 (re-formed 2010)
Former Names: Merthyr Tydfil FC
Nickname: 'The Martyrs'
Ground: Penydarren Park, Merthyr Tydfil, Mid Glamorgan CF47 8RF
Record Attendance: 1,593 (15/09/2023)
Colours: Black and White striped shirts, White shorts
Telephone Nº: (01685) 359074
Ground Capacity: 4,000
Seating Capacity: 1,500
Website: www.merthyrtownfc.co.uk
E-mail: merthyrsec@gmail.com

GENERAL INFORMATION

Car Parking: At the ground and street parking
Coach Parking: Georgetown
Nearest Railway Station: Merthyr Tydfil (½ mile)
Nearest Bus Station: Merthyr Tydfil
Club Shop: At the ground
Opening Times: Weekdays 9.00am to 4.00pm and Matchdays
Telephone Nº: (01685) 359074

GROUND INFORMATION

Away Supporters' Entrances & Sections: Theatre End entrances and accommodation

ADMISSION INFO (2024/2025 PRICES)

Adult Standing/Seating: £13.00
Concessionary Standing/Seating: £10.00
Under-16s Standing/Seating: £3.00

DISABLED INFORMATION

Wheelchairs: 20 spaces are available in total in front of the Main Grandstand
Helpers: Please phone the club for information
Prices: Please phone the club for information
Disabled Toilets: Available in the Clubhouse
Contact: (01685) 359074 (Bookings are not necessary)

Travelling Supporters' Information:
Routes: From the East: Take the A470 to Merthyr. At the top of Merthyr High Street. take a sharp left at the lights and then 1st right into Brecon Road. Take the 1st right and then 1st right once again and follow the road into the ground; From the North: Leave the A465 Heads of the Valleys road for Dowlais. After approximately 2 miles, fork right into Brecon Road. Take the 1st right then 1st right once again and follow the road into the ground.

PLYMOUTH PARKWAY FC

Founded: 1988
Former Names: Ex-Air Flyers FC
Nickname: 'The Parkway'
Ground: Bolitho Park, St. Peter's Road, Manadon, Plymouth PL5 3JH
Record Attendance: 1,385 (v Truro City 26/12/2022)

Colours: Yellow shirts and Blue shorts
Ground Capacity: 3,500
Seating Capacity: 250
Website: www.ppfc.co.uk
E-mail: Via the form on the club's website

GENERAL INFORMATION

Car Parking: Limited parking at the ground
Coach Parking: At the ground
Nearest Railway Station: Plymouth
Club Shop: None

GROUND INFORMATION

Away Supporters' Entrances & Sections:
No usual segregation

ADMISSION INFO (2024/2025 PRICES)

Adult Standing/Seating: £12.00
Concessionary Standing/Seating: £10.00
Ages 10 to 16 Standing/Seating: £7.00
Note: Children aged 10 to 16 must be accompanied by a paying adult.

DISABLED INFORMATION

Wheelchairs: Accommodated
Helpers: Admitted
Prices: Normal prices apply for the disabled and helpers
Disabled Toilets: Available
Contact: Via e-mail (Bookings are recommended)

Travelling Supporters' Information:
Routes: Exit the A38 Devon Expressway Plymouth at the Manadon (A386) turn-off and follow St. Peter's Road past Manadon Vale Primary School on the right. Continue along St. Peter's Road for approximately 1 mile and Bolitho Park is situated on the right near the junction with Shakespeare Road.

POOLE TOWN FC

Founded: 1880
Former Names: Various names including Poole FC and Poole St. Marys FC
Nickname: 'The Dolphins'
Ground: Black Gold Stadium, School Lane, Oakdale, Poole BH15 3JR
Record Attendance: 2,203 (2015)

Colours: Red & White halved shirts with Red shorts
Ground Capacity: 2,500
Seating Capacity: 268
Website: www.pooletownfc.co.uk
E-mail: Via the form on the club's website

GENERAL INFORMATION

Car Parking: At the ground
Coach Parking: At the ground
Nearest Railway Station: Poole (¾ mile)
Nearest Bus Station: Poole
Club Shop: At the ground
Opening Times: Matchdays only

GROUND INFORMATION

Away Supporters' Entrances & Sections:
No usual segregation

ADMISSION INFO (2024/2025 PRICES)

Adult Standing/Seating: £12.00
Senior Citizen Standing/Seating: £8.00
Under-18s Standing/Seating: £5.00
Under-13s Standing/Seating: £1.00

DISABLED INFORMATION

Wheelchairs: Accommodated
Helpers: Admitted
Prices: Normal prices apply for the disabled and helpers
Disabled Toilets: One available
Contact: Via e-mail (Bookings are not necessary)

Travelling Supporters' Information:
Routes: Take the A35, A3049 or the A349 into Poole to the Fleetsbridge Interchange where these roads all meet. At the interchange, takes the Fleets Lane exit and head southwards into the centre of Poole. Continue along Fleets Lane into Stanley Green Road (passing the Retail Park and part of the Industrial Estate) for approximately ½ mile then turn left into Palmer Road. Take the first turning on the right into School Lane for the ground.

SHOLING FC

Founded: 1884 (re-formed 1960)
Former Names: Vosper Thornycroft FC, VT FC and a number of other earlier names
Nickname: 'The Boatmen'
Ground: Mortgage Decisions Stadium, Portsmouth Road, Old Netley, Southampton SO19 9PW
Record Attendance: 1,300 (vs Hamworthy Utd, 2023)
Colours: Red and White striped shirts with Black shorts
Ground Capacity: 2,500
Seating Capacity: 288
Website: www.sholingfc.co.uk
E-mail: admin@sholingfc.co.uk

GENERAL INFORMATION

Car Parking: At the ground
Coach Parking: Please contact the club
Nearest Railway Station: Sholing (1½ miles)
Club Shop: None

GROUND INFORMATION

Away Supporters' Entrances & Sections:
No usual segregation

ADMISSION INFO (2024/2025 PRICES)

Adult Standing/Seating: £12.00
Concessionary Standing/Seating: £8.00
Note: Under-19s are admitted free of charge when accompanied by a paying adult

DISABLED INFORMATION

Wheelchairs: Accommodated
Helpers: Admitted
Prices: Normal prices apply for the disabled and helpers
Disabled Toilets: Available
Contact: Via e-mail (Bookings are not necessary)

Travelling Supporters' Information:
Routes: Exit the M27 at Junction 8 and take the 2nd exit at the roundabout into A3025 Hamble Lane. After approximately ½ mile, turn right into Portsmouth Road (still the A3025) and the ground is on the right hand side of the road after ½ mile.

SWINDON SUPERMARINE FC

Founded: 1992
Former Names: None
Nickname: 'Marine'
Ground: The Webswood Stadium, Supermarine Road, Swindon SN3 4BZ
Record Attendance: 1,550
Colours: Blue shirts and shorts
Telephone Nº: (01793) 828778
Ground Capacity: 3,000
Seating Capacity: 345
Website: www.swindonsupermarinefc.com
E-mail: supermarinefc@aol.com

GENERAL INFORMATION

Car Parking: 200 spaces at the ground (£1.00 charge per car)
Coach Parking: At the ground
Nearest Railway Station: Swindon (4 miles)
Club Shop: At the ground
Opening Times: Matchdays only
Telephone Nº: (01793) 828778

GROUND INFORMATION

Away Supporters' Entrances & Sections:
No usual segregation

ADMISSION INFO (2024/2025 PRICES)

Adult Standing/Seating: £12.00
Concession Standing/Seating: £8.00
Ages 12 to 17 Standing/Seating: £6.00
Note: Under-12s are admitted free of charge when accompanied by a paying adult.

DISABLED INFORMATION

Wheelchairs: Accommodated
Helpers: Admitted
Prices: Normal prices apply for the disabled and helpers
Disabled Toilets: Available
Contact: (01793) 828778 (Bookings are not necessary)

Travelling Supporters' Information:
Routes: The ground is located next to the South Marston Industrial Estate just off the A361 to the north of Swindon and south of Highworth. Follow the signs for the Industrial Estate then turn into Supermarine Road at the roundabout to the north of the industrial estate. The ground is on the left hand side of the road, opposite the industrial estate.

TAUNTON TOWN FC

Founded: 1947
Former Names: None
Nickname: 'The Peacocks'
Ground: The Cygnet Health Care Stadium, Wordsworth Drive, Taunton TA1 2HG
Record Attendance: 3,284 (1999)

Colours: Claret shirts with Sky Blue shorts
Telephone Nº: (01823) 254909
Ground Capacity: 3,000
Seating Capacity: 422
Website: www.tauntontown.com
E-mail: admin@tauntontown.com

GENERAL INFORMATION

Car Parking: At the ground
Coach Parking: At the ground
Nearest Railway Station: Taunton (1¼ miles)
Club Shop: None

GROUND INFORMATION

Away Supporters' Entrances & Sections:
No usual segregation

ADMISSION INFO (2024/2025 PRICES)

Adult Standing/Seating: £14.00
Concessions Standing/Seating: £11.00
Ages 6 to 16 Standing/Seating: £5.00
Under-6s are admitted free with paying Adult

DISABLED INFORMATION

Wheelchairs: Accommodated
Helpers: Admitted
Prices: Normal prices apply for the disabled. Helpers pay concessionary prices
Disabled Toilets: Available
Contact: (01823) 254909 (Bookings are not necessary)

Travelling Supporters' Information:
Routes: Exit the M5 at Junction 25 and follow signs for Taunton Town Centre. Bear left at the first set of traffic lights then go straight on at the next set of traffic lights into Wordsworth Drive. The ground is on the left hand side of the road after approximately 200 yards.

TIVERTON TOWN FC

Founded: 1913
Former Names: Tiverton Athletic FC
Nickname: 'Tivvy, Yellows and Gold Army'
Ground: Ian Moorcroft Stadium, Ladysmead, Bolham Road, Tiverton EX16 6SG
Record Attendance: 3,000 (vs Leyton Orient 1994)
Colours: Yellow & Black shirts and shorts
Telephone N°: (01884) 252397
Ground Capacity: 3,500
Seating Capacity: 520
Website: www.tivertontownfc.co.uk
E-mail: Via the form on the club's website

GENERAL INFORMATION

Car Parking: At the ground
Coach Parking: At the ground
Nearest Railway Station: Tiverton Parkway (7 miles)
Nearest Bus Station: Tiverton
Club Shop: At the ground
Opening Times: Matchdays only
Telephone N°: (01884) 252397

GROUND INFORMATION

Away Supporters' Entrances & Sections:
No usual segregation

ADMISSION INFO (2024/2025 PRICES)

Adult Standing/Seating: £11.00
Concessionary Standing/Seating: £8.00
Under-16s Standing/Seating: £1.00 (with paying adult)

DISABLED INFORMATION

Wheelchairs: Accommodated
Helpers: Admitted
Prices: Normal prices apply
Disabled Toilets: Available
Contact: (01884) 252397 (Bookings are not necessary)

Travelling Supporters' Information:
Routes: Exit the M5 at Junction 27 and follow the A361 towards Tiverton for about 7 miles. Ignore the first junction for the A396 (Tiverton and Bickleigh) at Gornhay Cross and keep going until you reach a large roundabout. Turn left at the roundabout (A3126) for the Town Centre and Castle and continue along for about 400 yards. Cross the new roundabout passing the College Sports Field and Rugby Club and the ground is then on the right just by R & M Cars.

WALTON & HERSHAM FC

Founded: 1896
Former Names: Walton FC and Hersham FC
Nickname: 'The Swans', 'The Sham' and 'The Waltz'
Ground: Elmbridge XCel Sports Hub,
Waterside Drive, Walton-on-Thames KT12 2JP
Record Attendance: 2,095 (vs Hanworth Villa, 2023)

Colours: Shirts and shorts are Red with White trim
Ground Capacity: 2,097
Seating Capacity: 318
Website: www.waltonhershamfc.com
E-mail: info@waltonhershamfc.com

GENERAL INFORMATION

Car Parking: available at the Hub
Coach Parking: At the Hub
Nearest Railway Station: Walton-on-Thames (1¾ miles)
Buses: Take the 461 service to Waterside Drive
Club Shop: Online sales only

GROUND INFORMATION

Away Supporters' Entrances & Sections:
No usual segregation

ADMISSION INFO (2024/2025 PRICES)

Adult Standing/Seating: £12.00
Concessionary Standing/Seating: £9.00
Ages 13 to 21 Standing/Seating: £6.00
Under-13s Standing/Seating: £2.00 (with a paying adult)

DISABLED INFORMATION

Wheelchairs: Accommodated
Helpers: One helper per disabled fan
Prices: Normal prices for disabled but helpers free
Disabled Toilets: Within the Hub
Contact: Via e-mail (Bookings are not necessary)

Travelling Supporters' Information:
Routes: The Elmbridge Xcel Sports Hub is located on the southern side of the Thames next to the B.P. Amoco Oil Terminal and is accessed via the A3050 (Terrace Road/Hurst Road) at the roundabout next to Grovelands Primary School.

WIMBORNE TOWN FC

Founded: 1878
Former Names: None
Nickname: 'The Magpies'
Ground: The Wyatt Homes (New Cuthbury) Stadium, 16 Ainsley Road, Wimborne BH21 2FU
Record Attendance: 2,307 (vs Frome Town 2024)
Colours: Black & White striped shirts with Black shorts
Telephone Nº: (01202) 884821
Ground Capacity: 2,800
Seating Capacity: 300
Website: www.wimbornetownfc.co.uk

GENERAL INFORMATION
Car Parking: At the ground
Coach Parking: At the ground
Nearest Railway Station: Hamworth (9½ miles)
Club Shop: At the ground
Opening Times: Matchdays only
Telephone Nº: (01202) 884821

GROUND INFORMATION
Away Supporters' Entrances & Sections:
No usual segregation

ADMISSION INFO (2024/2025 PRICES)
Adult Standing/Seating: £14.00
Concessionary Standing/Seating: £8.00
Under-18s Standing/Seating: £5.00
Under-13s Standing/Seating: £2.00

DISABLED INFORMATION
Wheelchairs: Accommodated
Helpers: Admitted
Prices: Normal prices apply for the disabled and helpers
Disabled Toilets: Available
Contact: (01202) 884821 (Bookings are not necessary)

Travelling Supporters' Information:
Routes: The ground is located on the southern outskirts of Wimborne just to the north of the A31. Take the A31 to the junction with the B3073 at Canford Bottom roundabout then head into Wimborne along the B3073 (Wimborne Road West). After passing Hayes Lane on the right, turn left into Lonsdale Road and continue to the end which is a T-junction with Ainsley Road. Turn left at the junction and the entrance to the ground is on the right after a short distance.

WINCHESTER CITY FC

Founded: 1891
Former Names: Winchester Swallows FC and Winchester FC
Nickname: 'The Citizens'
Ground: Charters Community Stadium, Hillier Way, Abbotts Barton, Winchester SO23 7SU
Record Attendance: 1,023 (vs Bristol Manor 2022)

Colours: Red & Black striped shirts with Red shorts
Ground Capacity: 3,000
Seating Capacity: 250
Website: www.winchestercityfc.co.uk
E-mail: Via the form on the club's website

GENERAL INFORMATION

Car Parking: Spaces for 200 cars at the ground
Coach Parking: Coach Park (SatNav SO23 7AB)
Nearest Railway Station: Winchester (1 mile)
Club Shop: At the ground
Opening Times: Matchdays only 2.00pm to 6.00pm

GROUND INFORMATION

Away Supporters' Entrances & Sections:
No usual segregation

ADMISSION INFO (2024/2025 PRICES)

Adult Standing/Seating: £13.50
Concessionary Standing/Seating: £10.00
Ages 16 to 18 Standing/Seating: £6.00
Ages 12 to 15 Standing/Seating: £3.50
Under-12s Standing/Seating: Free with a paying adult

DISABLED INFORMATION

Wheelchairs: Accommodated
Helpers: Admitted
Prices: Normal prices apply for the disabled but helpers are admitted free of charge.
Disabled Toilets: Available
Contact: Via e-mail (Bookings are not necessary)

Travelling Supporters' Information:
Routes: Exit the M3 northbound at Junction 10 and take the B3330 Bar End Road into Winchester at the Bar End roundabout. At the next roundabout take the 1st exit onto Bridge Street then take the 2nd exit at the next roundabout along Eastgate, following the road to the left when it becomes Friargate (B3331). Turn right into Jewry Street then continue along Hyde Street before turning right into Worthy Road. Continue along then turn right onto Russell Road and right again before reaching Hillier Way for the Stadium.

Northern Premier League Premier Division 2023-2024 Season	Ashton United	Atherton Collieries	Bamber Bridge	Basford United	Bradford (Park Avenue)	FC United of Manchester	Gainsborough Trinity	Guiseley	Hyde United	Ilkeston Town	Lancaster City	Macclesfield	Marine	Matlock Town	Morpeth Town	Radcliffe	Stafford Rangers	Warrington Rylands 1906	Whitby Town	Workington	Worksop Town
Ashton United		4-3	2-2	1-0	2-1	1-2	2-0	1-1	2-1	1-2	5-0	0-2	1-3	5-0	4-3	0-2	2-1	0-0	4-1	2-2	2-0
Atherton Collieries	1-2		1-2	1-2	2-0	1-2	0-1	1-2	1-2	2-3	0-2	0-1	0-5	1-3	4-3	0-4	1-0	1-1	2-3	4-3	0-2
Bamber Bridge	1-3	3-1		5-2	1-1	3-3	1-3	0-2	2-0	1-4	2-1	2-1	1-7	2-1	3-3	1-5	0-2	2-2	3-2	3-0	1-1
Basford United	1-2	1-1	4-0		2-0	1-1	3-0	0-1	0-0	0-1	1-0	1-3	2-1	2-1	2-2	1-3	1-2	2-2	1-1	0-3	3-1
Bradford (Park Avenue)	1-1	1-2	0-3	2-1		2-4	3-3	0-1	0-3	4-1	2-3	0-2	1-3	2-3	2-0	2-3	1-0	1-2	1-1	1-2	1-2
FC United of Manchester	0-2	0-2	3-0	2-0	2-0		2-0	3-2	0-2	1-0	4-3	2-1	0-3	2-3	2-5	0-1	2-1	1-2	1-1	1-3	3-0
Gainsborough Trinity	2-2	4-1	1-1	3-0	2-1	1-3		4-0	4-1	0-1	1-0	1-3	0-0	5-3	0-2	3-2	2-1	1-1	2-0	4-2	2-0
Guiseley	0-1	3-2	2-0	2-1	2-2	3-1	0-1		2-2	1-2	2-3	1-2	4-2	4-0	4-1	1-0	2-0	0-2	1-3	4-3	2-4
Hyde United	2-2	3-2	2-2	1-0	5-0	2-1	2-2	1-1		2-0	0-3	1-3	2-1	2-1	2-1	3-1	1-1	0-0	1-2	2-0	3-1
Ilkeston Town	2-2	3-0	1-0	4-1	2-2	2-0	4-0	1-4	1-1		2-3	1-1	1-1	0-1	3-2	1-2	3-1	0-1	2-4	6-1	1-2
Lancaster City	2-1	3-2	3-2	1-0	2-2	0-0	2-1	2-2	0-4	0-4		3-0	0-2	1-0	3-2	1-2	2-0	0-0	2-1	1-1	0-0
Macclesfield	5-0	6-0	2-1	1-1	3-4	3-1	3-0	5-1	0-0	5-3	1-2		2-1	3-0	3-0	2-3	2-0	1-1	2-1	2-0	1-2
Marine	1-1	4-0	4-1	2-0	4-0	5-1	3-1	1-0	1-4	0-0	2-1	1-2		2-0	3-1	3-2	4-0	1-1	1-3	4-4	2-1
Matlock Town	5-1	3-0	0-0	2-0	5-2	3-0	0-4	2-1	3-2	1-2	2-1	1-2	0-1		1-1	4-0	1-3	2-4	1-5	2-2	0-0
Morpeth Town	3-3	2-1	1-3	2-2	2-1	3-0	2-0	1-1	1-5	2-0	2-0	2-0	1-0	3-3		2-3	6-0	1-3	0-1	3-0	4-0
Radcliffe	2-5	2-2	3-2	1-1	3-0	5-0	1-0	3-4	2-0	3-0	4-2	4-3	3-2	4-0	4-1		3-1	2-3	0-1	3-1	4-3
Stafford Rangers	0-1	2-0	1-1	0-1	0-0	3-2	4-0	2-1	1-2	0-2	2-4	1-3	0-2	2-4	0-3	0-3		0-2	1-0	1-0	0-2
Warrington Rylands	2-0	1-1	2-0	1-1	2-3	1-0	1-4	0-1	1-0	2-0	1-2	2-3	2-0	1-0	2-0	0-4	7-2		1-0	1-0	2-1
Whitby Town	1-3	2-0	2-0	3-0	1-1	1-2	0-1	1-2	2-1	3-0	1-1	2-0	1-1	1-0	3-1	1-2	1-0	1-3		1-1	2-4
Workington	5-0	2-3	2-2	5-3	0-2	2-1	2-3	2-1	0-1	4-1	2-1	0-0	0-3	2-1	2-2	1-4	2-1	2-2	0-0		3-3
Worksop Town	1-0	4-1	2-4	1-0	3-1	4-0	4-0	1-1	1-0	1-2	0-0	1-0	0-1	2-0	7-0	1-1	5-0	2-1	1-0	2-1	

Northern Premier League – Premier Division

Season 2023/2024

Radcliffe	**40**	**28**	**3**	**9**	**103**	**58**	**87**
Macclesfield	40	24	5	11	84	47	77
Marine	**40**	**23**	**7**	**10**	**87**	**44**	**76**
Warrington Rylands 1906	40	21	12	7	65	42	75
Worksop Town	40	21	7	12	72	49	70
Hyde United	40	19	10	11	68	48	67
Ashton United	40	19	10	11	73	63	67
Gainsborough Trinity	40	19	6	15	66	63	63
Lancaster City	40	18	8	14	60	62	62
Guiseley	40	18	7	15	69	63	61
Ilkeston Town	40	18	6	16	69	62	60
Whitby Town	40	17	8	15	60	50	56
Morpeth Town	40	14	8	18	76	81	50
FC United of Manchester	40	15	4	21	55	77	48
Matlock Town	40	14	5	21	62	77	47
Bamber Bridge	40	12	11	17	63	82	47
Workington	40	11	11	18	67	81	44
Basford United	40	9	10	21	44	65	37
Bradford (Park Avenue)	***40***	***7***	***9***	***24***	***50***	***85***	***30***
Stafford Rangers	***40***	***9***	***3***	***28***	***36***	***81***	***30***
Atherton Collieries	***40***	***7***	***4***	***29***	***47***	***96***	***25***

Whitby Town had 3 points deducted after fielding an ineligible player.
FC United of Manchester had 1 point deducted after fielding an ineligible player.

Marske United resigned from the league on 3rd January 2024 and their record was expunged.

Northern Premier League Division One West 2023-2024 season	1874 Northwich	Avro	Bootle	Chasetown	City of Liverpool	Clitheroe	Hanley Town	Hednesford Town	Kidsgrove Athletic	Leek Town	Mossley	Nantwich Town	Newcastle Town	Prescot Cables	Runcorn Linnets	Stalybridge Celtic	Trafford	Vauxhall Motors	Widnes	Witton Albion
1874 Northwich		1-2	0-4	1-1	0-2	1-4	0-1	0-1	2-6	0-3	1-3	0-1	0-1	0-1	0-5	0-0	0-4	2-0	1-0	1-2
Avro	2-0		1-3	0-2	0-1	1-2	0-0	1-1	1-1	2-1	0-0	1-0	0-3	2-0	1-2	3-2	1-1	1-0	1-1	0-1
Bootle	5-1	1-0		3-1	0-2	1-2	3-0	1-3	1-1	2-0	1-1	3-1	2-1	0-0	1-3	0-4	1-1	1-2	2-1	1-1
Chasetown	4-2	0-1	3-2		6-4	3-3	0-0	0-0	2-0	2-1	2-0	0-3	1-1	1-2	0-1	1-0	4-0	1-0	1-1	3-2
City of Liverpool	1-2	1-1	2-0	1-0		2-1	0-0	2-1	5-0	2-2	4-1	2-3	3-1	1-4	2-3	1-1	2-2	5-0	2-0	1-1
Clitheroe	4-0	2-2	1-2	4-1	2-0		3-4	3-1	1-1	1-4	6-3	0-0	2-1	1-1	1-1	0-1	0-1	2-0	0-1	0-3
Hanley Town	4-2	0-1	0-2	1-1	0-0	2-0		3-1	0-0	1-3	0-2	1-0	1-3	0-3	0-0	1-2	1-1	4-0	0-1	2-1
Hednesford Town	1-1	0-3	0-1	1-1	1-5	0-4	1-2		2-3	1-1	0-1	3-2	3-0	0-2	1-1	1-1	1-1	1-1	3-0	3-0
Kidsgrove Athletic	5-0	2-2	0-2	2-1	0-3	2-1	4-1	1-1		0-5	1-1	1-4	1-2	1-1	3-0	2-2	1-2	2-1	0-3	1-3
Leek Town	4-1	3-4	1-1	4-1	1-0	1-3	2-1	3-0	2-4		1-0	2-0	3-0	3-0	3-0	3-0	3-0	2-2	1-0	4-1
Mossley	1-1	0-0	1-2	2-1	0-1	1-1	2-1	1-0	3-2	1-3		0-0	1-2	2-1	0-3	2-0	1-0	1-2	1-0	1-1
Nantwich Town	2-0	1-1	2-2	1-0	1-2	1-2	3-0	4-3	3-1	1-3	2-1		0-1	1-1	3-1	4-2	4-0	3-0	0-2	1-0
Newcastle Town	0-1	0-1	0-2	1-2	1-1	1-1	0-0	0-1	3-1	1-2	2-1	1-0		3-0	1-0	3-4	2-2	1-0	1-3	1-2
Prescot Cables	1-0	0-1	2-0	1-0	2-1	0-2	1-1	1-1	2-1	0-1	5-3	1-0	1-0		2-2	2-0	5-1	1-1	1-1	4-1
Runcorn Linnets	1-0	2-1	0-1	1-2	1-2	5-1	0-1	3-0	1-0	5-0	2-0	0-0	1-1	2-1		1-0	0-0	2-0	3-2	4-2
Stalybridge Celtic	0-0	2-2	1-1	0-1	4-2	2-2	2-1	3-2	2-1	1-5	1-0	3-2	2-1	1-1	0-1		1-0	1-2	4-3	4-0
Trafford	2-2	2-4	0-1	1-2	0-1	2-2	0-0	1-0	1-2	0-0	1-1	2-1	2-1	0-1	2-2	1-1		0-1	1-1	0-4
Vauxhall Motors	3-1	1-3	2-3	0-1	3-2	2-1	0-2	3-2	3-2	3-3	0-3	3-1	3-1	0-3	2-4	3-1	1-2		2-3	2-2
Widnes	5-0	2-0	2-0	1-0	1-1	1-2	0-1	5-1	2-0	0-1	4-0	1-2	0-2	4-2	2-0	1-1	2-0	2-1		1-3
Witton Albion	3-0	2-2	2-2	2-0	1-0	1-2	2-0	3-2	3-1	3-1	2-1	1-4	1-0	2-3	1-0	3-0	0-4	1-2	2-1	

Northern Premier League – Division One West

Season 2023/2024

Leek Town	**38**	**24**	**6**	**8**	**85**	**44**	**78**
Runcorn Linnets	38	20	8	10	63	39	68
Prescot Cables	**38**	**19**	**10**	**9**	**59**	**41**	**67**
Bootle	38	19	9	10	60	45	66
City of Liverpool	38	18	9	11	69	47	63
Witton Albion	38	19	6	13	65	59	63
Avro	38	15	13	10	49	43	58
Clitheroe	38	16	10	12	69	56	58
Widnes	38	17	6	15	60	43	57
Nantwich Town	38	17	6	15	61	47	57
Chasetown	38	16	8	14	52	50	56
Stalybridge Celtic	38	14	11	13	56	59	53
Hanley Town	38	12	11	15	37	46	47
Newcastle Town	38	13	6	19	44	51	45
Mossley	38	12	9	17	43	56	45
Vauxhall Motors	38	13	5	20	51	73	44
Trafford	38	8	15	15	40	57	39
Kidsgrove Athletic	38	10	9	19	56	74	39
Hednesford Town	***38***	***7***	***11***	***20***	***44***	***68***	***32***
1874 Northwich	***38***	***4***	***6***	***28***	***24***	***89***	***18***

Northern Premier League Division One East 2023-2024 Season	Ashington AFC	Belper Town	Bridlington Town	Brighouse Town	Carlton Town	Cleethorpes Town	Consett AFC	Dunston	Grantham Town	Grimsby Borough	Hebburn Town	Liversedge	Newton Aycliffe	North Ferriby	Ossett United	Pontefract Collieries	Sheffield	Stocksbridge Park Steels	Stockton Town	Winterton Rangers
Ashington AFC		1-0	5-2	4-4	4-0	1-2	0-2	3-1	0-1	1-2	4-0	0-2	2-4	2-0	0-1	2-1	1-3	1-1	1-4	0-0
Belper Town	2-2		2-0	1-3	4-0	0-5	2-1	3-4	5-0	1-1	0-3	1-0	3-4	2-1	2-0	1-3	2-1	0-0	0-4	3-1
Bridlington Town	2-0	1-5		3-0	0-1	2-3	3-0	0-3	2-2	2-2	0-1	1-0	3-5	2-1	1-2	0-0	1-2	4-0	2-2	2-0
Brighouse Town	3-3	0-2	2-2		2-0	2-2	3-1	0-2	4-2	0-0	0-2	3-2	2-1	3-3	0-1	1-4	0-1	1-1	1-3	1-5
Carlton Town	2-0	2-1	5-0	3-0		1-0	2-1	1-3	2-1	1-2	1-3	1-3	0-3	1-2	3-0	0-0	2-1	0-2	1-2	2-1
Cleethorpes Town	1-0	2-0	3-0	2-1	2-0		1-3	1-3	1-1	0-3	1-1	0-0	2-0	1-2	2-0	0-1	2-1	0-0	0-0	4-0
Consett AFC	2-3	0-1	1-1	0-2	2-1	3-2		0-2	3-2	2-0	3-0	2-2	1-1	3-1	1-2	0-2	4-1	1-0	2-2	0-0
Dunston	4-1	3-1	3-1	3-1	2-3	4-0	0-0		1-1	3-0	0-1	1-0	2-1	2-3	2-0	2-0	3-3	2-2	0-0	1-2
Grantham Town	2-2	2-3	2-3	3-1	2-3	2-2	1-0	1-1		1-2	0-4	0-1	3-2	2-4	2-1	2-2	0-0	2-1	0-4	1-2
Grimsby Borough	1-2	0-3	0-1	3-2	0-3	1-0	2-2	1-2	1-2		0-3	2-0	2-0	3-0	1-1	1-2	4-0	3-2	0-2	1-2
Hebburn Town	4-1	4-0	2-0	6-0	3-0	0-0	3-1	4-0	1-0	2-1		0-2	2-2	2-0	0-1	3-3	4-0	1-0	2-1	4-1
Liversedge	2-0	0-2	4-2	0-1	2-1	0-3	1-2	2-1	1-2	1-3	0-2		5-0	0-0	3-0	0-1	3-2	2-2	3-2	5-1
Newton Aycliffe	2-0	1-2	1-1	2-1	1-3	3-3	1-4	2-5	4-1	2-1	2-1	2-0		1-0	1-3	2-2	1-0	2-1	3-0	2-0
North Ferriby	0-5	0-4	3-1	2-0	1-4	2-1	3-2	0-1	4-2	0-1	1-0	0-2	4-1		3-1	1-0	1-0	3-1	0-1	3-0
Ossett United	1-2	1-1	1-1	1-1	0-2	1-2	3-1	2-4	0-0	0-2	4-4	0-4	3-4	1-0		0-4	1-4	0-0	0-1	4-2
Pontefract Collieries	3-3	3-0	3-0	2-2	1-2	2-2	0-2	1-1	1-0	6-0	2-3	2-1	0-2	4-1	4-0		1-0	2-1	2-0	3-0
Sheffield	4-0	1-1	3-1	2-0	0-2	1-1	5-0	3-2	1-2	3-2	0-2	1-0	1-1	4-4	3-1	1-2		4-2	0-2	4-0
Stocksbridge Park Steels	1-2	1-1	0-0	3-0	0-0	2-0	3-2	0-0	2-2	1-2	1-2	3-0	1-0	0-1	0-1	1-0	2-1		0-1	2-1
Stockton Town	2-0	7-1	2-0	3-0	0-2	4-3	3-2	1-1	2-0	3-0	3-1	0-0	2-0	3-0	3-0	0-0	5-1	2-2		2-0
Winterton Rangers	0-4	0-2	1-0	1-2	1-2	0-2	1-2	0-3	2-0	2-1	2-2	0-0	1-2	2-3	0-0	1-4	2-0	2-1	1-0	

Northern Premier League – Division One East

Season 2023/2024

Hebburn Town	**38**	**25**	**6**	**7**	**82**	**37**	**81**
Stockton Town	**38**	**24**	**8**	**6**	**78**	**31**	**80**
Dunston UTS	38	21	9	8	77	45	72
Pontefract Collieries	38	20	10	8	73	38	70
Carlton Town	38	21	2	15	59	52	65
Belper Town	38	18	6	14	64	62	60
Newton Aycliffe	38	18	6	14	68	67	60
North Ferriby	38	18	3	17	57	65	57
Cleethorpes Town	38	15	11	12	58	47	56
Liversedge	38	15	6	17	53	46	51
Grimsby Borough	38	15	5	18	51	60	50
Consett	38	14	7	17	58	62	49
Sheffield	38	14	6	18	62	64	48
Ashington	38	13	7	18	62	68	46
Stocksbridge Park Steels	38	9	13	16	42	48	40
Ossett United	38	10	8	20	38	70	38
Grantham Town	38	9	10	19	49	75	37
Bridlington Town	38	9	9	20	47	72	36
Brighouse Town	***38***	***9***	***9***	***20***	***49***	***81***	***36***
Winterton Rangers	***38***	***10***	***5***	***23***	***37***	***74***	***35***

Northern Premier League Division One Midlands 2023-2024 Season	AFC Rushden & Diamonds	Anstey Nomads	Bedworth United	Boldmere St Michaels	Cambridge City	Coleshill Town	Corby Town	Coventry Sphinx	Gresley Rovers	Harborough Town	Hinckley LRFC	Loughborough Dynamo	Lye Town	Quorn	Rugby Town	Shepshed Dynamo	Spalding United	Sporting Khalsa	Sutton Coldfield Town	Walsall Wood
AFC Rushden & Diamonds		0-3	0-3	3-2	4-1	2-1	1-3	0-0	0-3	0-4	1-2	1-1	0-4	0-5	1-1	1-0	0-3	0-1	1-0	1-2
Anstey Nomads	2-1		1-1	2-1	1-2	3-1	2-2	5-1	3-0	3-1	3-0	2-1	2-2	2-2	6-0	2-1	2-2	3-1	2-1	2-1
Bedworth United	2-2	1-2		1-1	0-0	4-0	2-0	1-0	2-1	0-1	1-1	0-2	0-1	1-1	0-3	0-1	2-1	3-0	0-1	0-1
Boldmere St Michaels	2-2	2-3	1-1		4-0	0-1	2-3	3-1	5-1	0-1	0-2	3-0	3-0	3-0	0-3	1-3	0-3	1-0	0-1	0-2
Cambridge City	1-0	1-4	2-4	0-4		4-3	1-1	0-1	3-2	0-7	1-1	3-4	2-4	2-2	5-1	4-1	0-1	1-2	4-2	0-3
Coleshill Town	0-4	1-2	4-2	0-4	2-1		2-2	2-3	1-1	1-2	3-5	4-2	3-1	3-3	3-1	1-6	2-3	1-0	0-2	3-1
Corby Town	3-2	1-1	2-3	1-2	4-0	0-1		3-0	1-2	3-4	1-0	0-1	0-0	2-3	1-1	0-1	1-2	7-1	2-2	3-0
Coventry Sphinx	2-1	2-2	0-1	1-1	2-2	0-0	0-1		1-1	1-2	1-1	2-2	2-0	1-1	1-1	1-5	0-1	0-1	0-1	1-2
Gresley Rovers	2-0	0-6	0-3	2-2	0-1	3-0	1-6	1-1		0-6	0-0	1-4	1-0	1-2	1-1	1-0	2-2	3-0	0-1	1-2
Harborough Town	0-2	1-2	2-0	2-0	3-1	3-0	1-1	6-1	4-0		2-0	6-0	1-0	5-0	2-1	4-0	0-0	2-0	2-3	2-1
Hinckley LRFC	3-0	0-3	2-1	2-1	2-0	3-2	3-2	1-0	3-1	1-1		0-0	2-2	1-0	3-1	1-0	0-1	2-2	2-0	1-1
Loughborough Dynamo	3-0	0-1	1-2	2-0	1-0	2-1	2-2	2-3	4-2	0-4	2-2		0-0	2-3	3-2	1-1	3-1	0-2	4-2	4-0
Lye Town	2-1	1-1	0-3	3-2	2-1	3-1	1-1	1-1	2-0	0-3	2-3	5-0		2-1	4-2	1-3	2-0	0-1	2-0	3-0
Quorn	7-1	1-1	3-0	2-0	1-0	3-1	0-0	4-2	6-1	0-1	1-2	0-2	4-0		2-1	1-0	1-2	2-1	1-1	3-2
Rugby Town	0-2	0-1	1-1	1-5	2-1	0-2	0-6	1-2	2-0	1-0	1-4	1-2	0-2	1-4		3-1	1-5	1-3	1-0	4-0
Shepshed Dynamo	2-1	0-3	1-2	1-1	0-0	1-0	3-2	2-2	2-0	0-1	1-2	3-3	0-2	1-1	1-2		0-3	3-0	0-1	2-3
Spalding United	2-0	0-5	1-0	2-1	3-0	8-0	1-2	4-0	4-0	1-1	2-0	4-2	2-0	3-1	1-0	6-1		5-0	4-0	3-0
Sporting Khalsa	4-1	2-4	2-2	1-2	2-1	4-1	0-6	3-0	2-2	0-1	3-1	2-3	1-0	0-4	2-0	2-0	1-7		0-2	3-0
Sutton Coldfield Town	2-0	4-2	1-0	1-2	0-0	2-2	0-1	4-1	7-1	0-1	1-3	0-2	0-1	5-3	4-3	0-1	2-2	1-1		1-4
Walsall Wood	0-2	2-2	2-1	3-4	1-1	3-0	2-4	1-1	2-1	1-2	4-3	1-2	0-1	1-3	1-0	2-1	1-3	2-2	3-0	

Northern Premier League – Division One Midland

Season 2023/2024

Spalding United	**38**	**28**	**5**	**5**	**98**	**33**	**89**
Anstey Nomads	38	26	10	2	96	40	88
Harborough Town	**38**	**29**	**4**	**5**	**91**	**24**	**85**
Hinckley LRFC	38	20	10	8	64	48	70
Quorn	38	19	9	10	81	54	66
Loughborough Dynamo	38	18	8	12	69	66	62
Lye Town	38	18	7	13	56	47	61
Corby Town	38	15	11	12	80	50	56
Bedworth United	38	14	9	15	50	45	51
Sutton Coldfield Town	38	15	6	17	55	58	51
Walsall Wood	38	15	5	18	57	70	50
Sporting Khalsa	38	15	5	18	52	74	50
Boldmere St. Michaels	38	14	6	18	65	57	48
Shepshed Dynamo	38	12	6	20	49	61	42
Coleshill Town	38	10	5	23	53	93	35
Coventry Sphinx	38	6	14	18	38	70	32
Cambridge City	38	8	8	22	46	81	32
Rugby Town	38	9	5	24	45	82	32
AFC Rushden & Diamonds	***38***	***9***	***5***	***24***	***38***	***78***	***32***
Gresley Rovers	***38***	***7***	***8***	***23***	***39***	***91***	***29***

Harborough Town had 6 points deducted after fielding an ineligible player.

Isthmian League Premier Division 2023-2024 Season	Billericay Town	Bognor Regis Town	Canvey Island	Carshalton Athletic	Chatham Town	Cheshunt	Concord Rangers	Cray Wanderers	Dulwich Hamlet	Enfield Town	Folkestone Invicta	Haringey Borough	Hashtag United	Hastings United	Hornchurch	Horsham	Kingstonian	Lewes	Margate	Potters Bar Town	Whitehawk	Wingate & Finchley
Billericay Town		2-1	0-1	2-0	2-0	2-1	2-0	6-0	3-0	1-1	1-2	1-2	2-4	2-0	1-1	1-2	1-0	5-0	5-3	2-1	1-3	1-2
Bognor Regis Town	1-0		1-1	3-3	2-1	1-1	2-0	2-1	0-2	2-4	4-0	3-0	0-0	0-1	1-2	2-0	2-0	3-3	2-2	2-2	2-2	2-2
Canvey Island	3-0	1-3		0-0	3-2	1-1	1-0	2-1	0-2	0-3	2-1	3-2	2-2	0-0	4-1	1-2	3-2	0-2	4-1	1-4	1-2	0-2
Carshalton Athletic	1-2	3-3	0-3		2-0	1-4	2-0	1-2	3-0	1-1	3-1	1-0	0-1	2-1	2-2	1-2	4-1	1-1	3-0	5-0	2-1	2-3
Chatham Town	6-3	1-0	5-1	2-2		3-2	2-1	1-5	2-1	3-1	2-0	2-1	2-3	1-2	2-0	1-3	4-1	3-0	2-1	2-0	1-0	2-1
Cheshunt	0-1	3-1	1-3	1-0	1-2		2-1	0-1	2-1	1-2	3-2	0-2	1-1	2-3	0-6	1-0	5-4	4-0	0-1	2-4	2-0	0-1
Concord Rangers	2-1	0-4	1-3	1-2	1-3	0-3		0-3	1-2	0-1	2-1	0-0	1-4	3-3	0-3	1-1	0-0	4-1	1-2	0-2	1-1	0-2
Cray Wanderers	0-1	1-5	2-1	1-0	2-2	2-1	1-1		1-1	2-0	0-1	3-3	1-3	0-0	1-4	1-3	1-0	1-1	0-0	1-2	2-2	1-0
Dulwich Hamlet	1-2	1-1	4-1	2-1	2-5	4-2	2-0	2-6		0-4	3-1	3-1	2-1	1-2	2-3	1-1	3-2	2-0	2-2	2-2	0-0	3-0
Enfield Town	1-2	2-2	3-0	0-3	2-2	3-0	3-0	2-0	3-2		0-2	1-0	6-3	3-1	1-2	2-1	0-0	1-0	2-0	3-1	4-4	2-2
Folkestone Invicta	1-0	0-1	1-0	3-3	2-3	2-1	1-1	2-2	3-3	1-2		1-1	1-3	0-5	0-2	3-1	3-2	3-1	2-0	0-0	1-1	1-1
Haringey Borough	0-6	0-1	2-1	0-6	0-3	1-0	0-1	0-4	1-1	1-1	0-0		1-4	0-5	1-2	0-2	2-2	0-4	1-0	0-3	1-1	1-2
Hashtag United	2-1	4-5	3-1	2-2	1-1	3-3	2-3	1-0	2-2	3-3	0-0	5-0		1-2	0-3	1-2	2-2	2-3	4-2	2-3	1-1	2-0
Hastings United	1-1	1-1	0-2	4-0	1-1	1-1	3-0	3-0	2-2	0-3	2-1	2-1	2-0		1-0	0-2	3-2	1-3	4-0	0-1	0-1	2-3
Hornchurch	4-1	4-1	2-0	1-1	2-1	1-0	1-0	2-0	2-1	2-0	4-2	3-0	3-0	4-1		1-1	2-1	1-1	4-1	3-0	0-0	1-2
Horsham	0-0	5-4	2-1	1-2	2-2	1-0	2-0	2-0	3-2	1-1	2-1	1-0	0-2	2-1	1-2		3-1	1-3	1-0	2-0	0-1	1-1
Kingstonian	1-3	3-2	2-1	2-3	1-3	1-1	1-2	3-0	2-1	2-3	3-0	0-3	3-5	1-3	0-3	1-2		1-3	1-3	0-2	1-4	1-2
Lewes	0-3	1-0	2-2	1-3	0-3	2-1	2-1	1-0	0-2	4-0	1-3	4-1	2-1	3-1	2-2	2-1	2-1		4-2	3-0	1-1	1-2
Margate	1-3	0-2	3-2	0-1	2-0	1-2	1-1	1-1	1-4	1-1	0-2	1-1	1-1	1-2	0-1	1-3	2-2	2-0		2-1	2-1	2-1
Potters Bar Town	1-3	1-1	1-2	1-1	0-0	1-1	4-3	1-1	1-2	0-2	3-3	2-1	5-0	1-3	0-1	0-1	6-1	1-2	2-3		1-0	3-2
Whitehawk	0-1	3-2	0-2	1-0	1-2	2-0	4-0	2-0	1-1	1-0	3-2	2-1	1-1	0-0	0-4	3-1	3-0	1-2	3-2	2-1		3-3
Wingate & Finchley	2-1	0-1	6-2	3-0	4-2	3-2	2-0	1-3	2-3	1-4	0-4	1-0	0-0	2-2	1-4	2-0	2-1	3-0	1-0	3-1	5-1	

Isthmian League Premier Division

Season 2023/2024

Hornchurch	**42**	**31**	**7**	**4**	**95**	**34**	**100**
Chatham Town	42	24	7	11	87	61	79
Enfield Town	**42**	**22**	**11**	**9**	**81**	**54**	**77**
Wingate & Finchley	42	23	7	12	78	62	76
Horsham	42	23	7	12	64	50	76
Billericay Town	42	23	4	15	78	52	73
Hastings United	42	19	10	13	71	54	67
Lewes	42	20	7	15	68	70	67
Whitehawk	42	17	14	11	63	54	65
Bognor Regis Town	42	16	14	12	78	63	62
Carshalton Athletic	42	17	11	14	73	59	62
Dulwich Hamlet	42	17	11	14	77	72	62
Hashtag United	42	15	14	13	82	75	59
Canvey Island	42	16	6	20	62	74	54
Potters Bar Town	42	14	9	19	65	70	51
Folkestone Invicta	42	13	11	18	60	71	50
Cray Wanderers	42	13	11	18	54	66	50
Cheshunt	42	12	7	23	58	72	43
Margate	***42***	***10***	***9***	***23***	***50***	***80***	***39***
Haringey Borough	***42***	***6***	***9***	***27***	***32***	***88***	***27***
Concord Rangers	***42***	***6***	***8***	***28***	***34***	***82***	***26***
Kingstonian	42	5	6	31	55	102	21

Isthmian League North Division 2023-2024 Season	Basildon United	Bowers & Pitsea	Brentwood Town	Brightlingsea Regent	Bury Town	Enfield	Felixstowe & Walton	Gorleston	Grays Athletic	Heybridge Swifts	Ipswich Wanderers	Lowestoft Town	Maldon & Tiptree	New Salamis	Redbridge	Stowmarket Town	Walthamstow	Witham Town	Wroxham
Basildon United		1-2	0-1	2-1	1-3	2-0	2-4	2-1	2-1	1-2	0-1	1-1	2-1	1-0	2-1	4-2	2-3	4-0	1-0
Bowers & Pitsea	2-1		0-2	0-1	1-0	1-0	2-1	1-1	3-1	3-1	1-0	1-3	2-3	3-2	3-0	3-2	2-4	2-0	3-2
Brentwood Town	2-3	1-3		0-2	0-0	1-0	2-2	1-1	3-1	0-1	1-0	0-1	3-2	1-1	1-1	9-0	2-0	0-0	2-0
Brightlingsea Regent	1-2	4-1	2-0		1-4	3-1	0-2	0-1	2-1	2-2	4-1	2-1	3-0	1-0	3-3	2-0	2-3	1-3	2-3
Bury Town	2-6	2-2	2-1	1-2		6-0	3-3	2-2	3-1	3-1	4-3	4-1	1-0	2-1	2-0	4-1	4-0	3-0	0-0
Enfield	0-3	1-3	0-2	1-4	2-7		1-2	0-3	3-0	1-3	0-0	0-5	0-1	3-1	0-1	4-0	0-2	1-5	3-2
Felixstowe & Walton Utd	1-0	3-2	1-0	5-3	3-0	5-1		4-0	3-2	0-0	1-1	3-0	0-1	6-1	4-0	2-1	2-0	1-0	0-2
Gorleston	3-3	0-2	2-3	0-1	0-3	4-1	1-0		0-2	0-0	2-0	1-2	4-2	3-1	1-0	1-1	0-0	4-0	1-1
Grays Athletic	1-1	0-2	0-3	1-0	2-2	4-0	0-3	0-2		1-3	3-2	2-3	0-1	2-4	2-0	3-1	0-4	3-1	1-1
Heybridge Swifts	1-1	2-2	1-2	1-0	6-1	1-1	2-3	2-1	2-0		2-0	2-1	1-0	2-1	0-0	3-0	1-1	0-1	0-1
Ipswich Wanderers	2-1	0-2	1-6	0-7	2-0	0-1	1-2	1-2	1-4	1-2		2-1	1-2	2-0	0-5	2-2	0-2	2-0	0-2
Lowestoft Town	5-1	2-0	1-2	2-1	0-0	2-0	2-0	2-3	2-0	6-0	1-2		2-0	6-1	5-1	2-1	3-2	3-1	4-0
Maldon & Tiptree	3-2	0-3	1-3	2-0	2-4	3-2	2-2	2-0	1-1	1-3	2-0	2-3		2-2	4-2	5-1	4-0	3-4	5-1
New Salamis	4-0	1-1	0-3	4-2	0-5	3-2	1-1	2-0	3-2	0-3	3-2	1-3	1-1		1-2	5-1	1-3	1-2	1-2
Redbridge	1-0	2-3	1-3	1-1	1-2	3-0	0-1	1-0	4-1	2-1	1-4	2-4	4-3	3-3		2-1	2-3	2-0	0-0
Stowmarket Town	3-4	1-3	1-3	0-1	0-5	2-2	2-2	0-6	0-2	0-1	1-1	0-6	2-5	3-4	0-5		0-3	1-1	2-3
Walthamstow	4-2	1-2	1-2	0-2	1-1	1-0	1-1	4-2	1-1	5-1	2-1	2-2	1-0	2-2	0-2	3-1		0-0	2-0
Witham Town	1-5	2-4	1-3	0-1	0-2	1-1	3-2	3-2	2-0	3-0	2-2	1-2	3-2	2-2	1-1	8-0	3-0		2-2
Wroxham	2-1	2-0	0-1	3-2	1-2	0-1	1-3	0-1	1-1	0-0	4-0	0-2	1-0	3-0	1-1	6-1	0-2	0-0	

Isthmian League North Division

Season 2023/2024

Lowestoft Town	**36**	**25**	**3**	**8**	**91**	**41**	**78**
Bury Town	36	22	8	6	89	47	74
Felixstowe & Walton United	36	22	8	6	78	40	74
Bowers & Pitsea	**36**	**23**	**4**	**9**	**70**	**49**	**73**
Brentwood Town	36	22	6	8	69	33	72
Walthamstow	36	18	8	10	63	50	62
Heybridge Swifts	36	17	9	10	53	45	60
Brightlingsea Regent	36	18	3	15	66	51	57
Basildon United	36	16	4	16	66	62	52
Gorleston	36	14	8	14	55	49	50
Maldon & Tiptree	36	15	4	17	68	64	49
Wroxham	36	13	9	14	47	47	48
Redbridge	36	13	8	15	57	60	47
Witham Town	36	12	9	15	56	62	45
New Salamis	36	9	8	19	58	82	35
Grays Athletic	36	9	6	21	46	69	33
Ipswich Wanderers	36	8	5	23	38	75	29
Enfield	36	6	4	26	33	86	22
Stowmarket Town	***36***	***0***	***6***	***30***	***34***	***125***	***6***

East Thurrock United folded in September 2023 the club's playing record was expunged: 3 1 1 1 4 6 4

Isthmian League South Central Division 2023-2024 Season	Ascot United	Ashford Town	Badshot Lea	Binfield	Chertsey Town	Chipstead	Corinthian-Casuals	Guernsey	Hanworth Villa	Hartley Wintney	Leatherhead	Marlow	Metropolitan Police	Northwood	Raynes Park Vale	South Park	Southall	Sutton Common Rovers	Thatcham Town	Uxbridge	Westfield
Ascot United		2-2	3-1	4-0	1-2	1-0	2-2	4-0	1-3	0-2	0-1	0-2	0-2	1-0	2-3	2-0	1-3	1-1	1-5	2-2	0-3
Ashford Town	2-1		1-3	6-0	0-3	1-1	2-0	1-3	3-5	0-3	0-1	1-3	2-0	0-6	0-1	0-1	0-0	1-1	0-1	1-2	0-2
Badshot Lea	0-1	3-0		2-5	0-2	4-2	3-2	4-2	2-2	1-3	2-3	2-2	2-2	4-0	2-0	0-4	0-2	0-1	2-2	2-0	0-4
Binfield	2-3	0-1	0-3		1-1	1-1	4-1	1-2	0-3	2-5	0-2	1-2	1-1	6-3	0-0	1-1	1-0	2-0	3-5	1-1	2-3
Chertsey Town	3-1	2-1	2-1	9-0		2-1	4-1	4-1	2-1	2-1	2-1	1-0	3-0	0-0	4-1	4-4	2-1	0-0	2-2	2-1	1-1
Chipstead	1-0	2-2	0-0	0-5	1-2		4-1	4-1	0-0	6-2	0-4	1-2	0-2	1-3	1-4	1-4	0-1	2-3	0-3	2-0	0-1
Corinthian-Casuals	1-2	1-2	1-3	0-0	0-6	0-1		0-4	1-0	0-3	2-3	1-4	2-1	2-1	1-2	0-2	1-1	0-5	1-3	4-2	1-1
Guernsey	2-4	0-1	1-3	3-3	2-6	5-3	1-1		0-5	2-3	1-4	0-1	1-1	3-3	2-3	0-1	0-3	4-2	3-1	3-0	3-1
Hanworth Villa	2-2	4-1	3-1	1-1	1-2	3-1	2-1	4-4		1-3	2-1	2-3	0-1	2-1	1-3	2-0	3-3	2-1	1-1	1-0	4-2
Hartley Wintney	1-0	1-0	0-1	1-4	1-3	0-2	1-1	2-0	2-1		1-1	0-4	5-2	4-0	1-1	0-0	0-3	2-1	2-2	1-3	0-4
Leatherhead	1-0	1-0	1-2	2-0	0-1	1-1	1-0	1-0	1-1	3-0		0-2	2-1	0-0	4-1	5-1	2-1	1-0	5-0	4-0	0-0
Marlow	2-1	3-0	1-0	8-1	0-1	4-0	4-1	2-4	3-1	2-3	4-0		4-0	4-1	2-1	2-2	1-2	6-1	0-1	3-2	1-2
Metropolitan Police	2-5	0-2	1-1	1-2	0-1	4-0	3-0	2-1	1-1	2-2	0-4	1-2		0-0	0-1	2-1	1-2	0-4	0-1	0-0	0-3
Northwood	2-3	1-3	6-1	4-1	2-4	0-1	4-0	2-1	2-3	3-0	1-2	1-3	1-0		2-2	0-3	1-2	5-1	4-1	3-0	1-2
Raynes Park Vale	3-2	2-1	1-4	4-0	3-2	2-1	2-0	5-4	0-0	1-1	0-1	1-4	0-0	1-0		1-1	2-0	0-0	2-1	2-0	4-0
South Park	4-1	3-0	2-2	2-1	0-4	2-1	2-0	1-1	1-1	6-2	1-2	1-2	0-0	2-0	0-3		3-1	2-1	5-1	1-1	4-5
Southall	0-1	2-1	3-1	8-0	0-3		5-2	1-1	4-1	2-0	1-0	4-1	1-2	2-1	0-1	3-2		1-0	1-0	3-1	3-1
Sutton Common Rovers	1-0	1-4	1-1	4-1	0-2	2-0	2-0	2-1	1-2	1-5	0-1	0-3	2-0	2-2	1-2	3-0	1-2		1-3	1-2	0-3
Thatcham Town	2-0	2-0	0-1	3-2	1-1	3-0	1-2	4-1	1-3	2-0	0-2	4-5	0-2	2-0	0-0	3-0	2-2	1-0		4-1	2-2
Uxbridge	1-1	3-0	3-0	2-2	0-6	2-1	5-0	2-0	1-3	5-0	1-3	1-3	2-0	4-2	4-2	1-2	2-3	4-0	3-1		1-2
Westfield	1-0	0-0	1-1	7-2	0-0	3-1	3-0	2-1	1-0	5-1	3-0	3-2	2-0	2-1	0-3	2-1	1-3	1-1	2-1	0-5	

Isthmian League South Central Division

Season 2023/2024

Chertsey Town	**40**	**31**	**8**	**1**	**103**	**32**	**100**
Marlow	**40**	**29**	**2**	**9**	**106**	**49**	**89**
Leatherhead	40	27	5	8	71	32	86
Westfield	40	25	8	7	81	50	83
Southall	39	25	5	9	79	43	80
Raynes Park Vale	40	23	9	8	70	49	78
Hanworth Villa	40	18	11	11	77	59	65
Thatcham Town	40	18	8	14	72	62	62
South Park	40	17	10	13	72	61	61
Hartley Wintney	40	16	7	17	64	79	55
Badshot Lea	40	15	9	16	65	70	54
Uxbridge	40	15	6	19	70	71	51
Ascot United	40	13	6	21	56	67	45
Sutton Common Rovers	40	11	7	22	49	69	40
Northwood	40	11	6	23	69	75	39
Metropolitan Police	40	9	10	21	37	63	37
Ashford Town	40	10	6	24	42	70	36
Guernsey	40	9	7	24	68	97	34
Binfield	40	8	10	22	59	109	34
Chipstead	***39***	***8***	***6***	***25***	***44***	***80***	***30***
Corinthian-Casuals	***40***	***5***	***6***	***29***	***34***	***101***	***21***

Chertsey Town had one point deducted after fielding an ineligible player.

Isthmian League South East Division 2023-2024 Season	Ashford United	Beckenham Town	Broadbridge Heath	Burgess Hill Town	Chichester City	Cray Valley Paper Mills	East Grinstead Town	Erith & Belvedere	Herne Bay	Horndean	Hythe Town	Lancing	Littlehampton Town	Merstham	Phoenix Sports	Ramsgate	Sevenoaks Town	Sheppey United	Sittingbourne	Three Bridges
Ashford United		3-2	2-3	1-0	1-3	0-2	0-1	4-1	3-1	3-1	0-1	3-4	1-0	3-2	3-5	2-3	2-1	3-2	1-5	3-2
Beckenham Town	0-1		0-4	0-4	0-2	0-6	3-0	1-1	3-3	3-1	5-2	2-3	1-6	2-1	1-2	2-5	2-2	4-2	2-3	1-2
Broadbridge Heath	1-0	3-3		0-0	0-3	2-3	0-1	1-0	1-1	1-1	2-0	2-2	2-0	6-6	3-1	0-2	4-2	2-2	0-2	3-0
Burgess Hill Town	3-0	1-0	0-0		3-5	1-4	3-0	0-2	2-1	1-0	1-2	2-4	1-1	5-1	2-2	1-2	1-0	1-2	1-1	2-3
Chichester City	1-2	4-0	2-1	3-0		0-3	7-1	6-1	1-3	1-3	5-0	3-0	2-0	1-1	1-3	2-4	1-0	2-0	0-2	0-1
Cray Valley Paper Mills	2-0	2-1	2-2	5-0	0-0		4-1	3-0	4-2	1-1	2-0	1-1	2-2	4-1	3-1	1-1	2-1	3-1	2-2	4-5
East Grinstead Town	6-0	1-1	1-1	1-5	1-1	0-4		1-1	1-2	4-0	2-3	0-2	5-1	4-1	1-1	2-6	0-3	1-2	1-2	1-2
Erith & Belvedere	0-1	0-2	1-2	2-2	1-1	1-3	0-4		1-1	1-2	1-0	0-3	2-1	3-1	1-0	0-5	0-1	0-4	0-4	0-2
Herne Bay	2-2	3-2	3-1	2-2	3-3	0-1	3-2	0-0		4-3	1-2	3-1	4-1	2-0	2-0	1-2	1-2	1-2	0-3	3-3
Horndean	2-1	4-1	4-0	1-0	0-3	0-2	1-3	2-0	2-4		0-4	1-1	2-1	1-3	4-4	1-0	3-0	2-5	0-3	1-3
Hythe Town	2-2	1-2	2-1	2-2	0-2	0-4	4-0	1-3	1-3	0-4		1-1	1-0	0-1	0-1	2-2	4-0	2-2	0-1	1-1
Lancing	4-2	1-1	2-1	0-1	0-4	0-1	3-0	3-1	0-3	4-1	2-1		3-2	1-0	4-2	4-2	1-2	1-2	0-0	4-0
Littlehampton Town	1-0	2-1	2-1	4-1	0-3	0-5	1-2	1-1	1-2	1-1	4-4	0-1		2-1	2-1	1-2	1-5	0-6	1-1	0-0
Merstham	2-2	4-3	0-1	3-1	0-3	0-1	1-1	2-0	2-2	1-1	0-2	1-2	0-1		3-0	0-3	5-0	3-2	0-1	3-2
Phoenix Sports	3-1	3-3	0-4	2-2	0-0	2-7	0-0	0-0	0-2	1-0	0-4	1-2	0-2	2-1		0-2	3-2	3-1	1-2	2-6
Ramsgate	4-0	1-0	1-0	4-2	4-0	2-2	5-0	4-1	3-1	2-0	3-1	7-2	4-0	0-2	9-1		1-0	0-0	2-2	1-2
Sevenoaks Town	1-2	1-1	0-1	3-3	1-0	0-1	4-1	3-0	1-2	3-2	0-0	4-2	2-1	2-2	1-2	4-2		0-1	2-2	2-2
Sheppey United	5-1	2-0	1-0	0-0	1-3	0-2	3-0	3-0	2-2	2-3	3-0	3-0	2-1	0-1	4-0	0-1	3-4		3-3	1-0
Sittingbourne	1-0	4-0	0-1	5-0	0-3	2-3	2-0	6-0	2-0	3-0	0-1	2-2	1-4	3-0	2-1	2-3	2-1	2-2		4-1
Three Bridges	3-2	3-2	4-2	2-3	3-2	0-2	4-2	6-1	1-1	2-2	8-3	4-1	3-1	3-3	4-2	0-2	2-1	6-0	3-0	

Isthmian League South East Division

Season 2023/2024

Cray Valley Paper Mills	**38**	**29**	**8**	**1**	**103**	**32**	**95**
Ramsgate	38	28	5	5	106	41	89
Sittingbourne	38	22	9	7	82	41	75
Three Bridges	38	22	7	9	98	68	73
Chichester City	**38**	**21**	**6**	**11**	**83**	**43**	**69**
Lancing	38	19	7	12	71	66	64
Sheppey United	38	18	7	13	76	57	61
Herne Bay	38	16	11	11	74	63	59
Broadbridge Heath	38	14	10	14	59	56	52
Sevenoaks Town	38	13	7	18	61	65	46
Ashford United	38	14	3	21	57	82	45
Burgess Hill Town	38	11	11	16	59	70	44
Hythe Town	38	12	8	18	54	71	44
Horndean	38	12	7	19	57	76	43
Merstham	38	11	8	19	58	72	41
Phoenix Sports	38	10	8	20	52	91	38
Littlehampton Town	38	10	7	21	49	76	37
East Grinstead Town	38	9	7	22	52	86	34
Beckenham Town	***38***	***7***	***8***	***23***	***57***	***93***	***29***
Erith & Belvedere	***38***	***6***	***8***	***24***	***27***	***86***	***26***

Southern Football League Premier Division Central 2023-2024 season	AFC Sudbury	AFC Telford United	Alvechurch	Barwell	Berkhamsted	Bromsgrove Sporting	Coalville Town	Halesowen Town	Hitchin Town	Kettering Town	Leamington	Leiston	Long Eaton United	Mickleover	Needham Market	Redditch United	Royston Town	St Ives Town	Stamford	Stourbridge	Stratford Town
AFC Sudbury		1-0	0-1	1-1	1-1	2-0	2-1	2-2	1-0	0-1	0-1	1-1	7-1	1-2	1-0	0-4	1-1	2-4	1-2	1-2	0-0
AFC Telford United	3-2		1-0	2-1	6-2	0-0	1-1	0-0	0-0	4-0	1-0	0-0	2-0	1-2	0-2	3-0	3-0	2-1	2-1	2-1	2-1
Alvechurch	1-0	0-2		4-4	1-1	1-0	1-4	0-2	2-1	1-1	1-0	0-2	2-1	1-2	0-3	4-4	1-0	1-4	4-3	1-0	1-0
Barwell	0-0	3-1	2-2		1-1	2-1	0-0	2-0	2-0	3-2	0-2	2-3	3-0	1-2	1-2	3-3	2-1	3-4	4-4	3-1	1-0
Berkhamsted	0-4	0-1	2-2	2-1		2-1	0-0	0-1	1-2	2-3	0-2	0-0	0-1	0-1	2-3	1-2	0-3	0-2	2-2	0-1	2-2
Bromsgrove Sporting	0-2	1-2	1-1	0-1	1-1		1-4	3-1	2-1	1-2	0-3	0-0	4-1	1-1	3-0	1-2	0-1	2-0	0-2	1-0	1-2
Coalville Town	0-3	1-4	2-1	3-1	9-0	1-0		1-1	1-0	3-1	5-2	1-2	1-1	1-0	1-6	2-0	1-1	0-1	1-2	0-0	1-1
Halesowen Town	4-1	0-2	1-0	1-1	2-1	2-1	2-1		1-3	1-2	0-0	2-1	5-0	2-1	0-1	1-2	0-3	4-3	2-0	1-0	2-0
Hitchin Town	2-1	1-1	2-0	0-0	1-3	1-2	4-3	0-1		0-1	1-2	1-4	2-3	2-2	0-2	2-2	1-2	3-2	1-2	0-0	3-4
Kettering Town	2-0	1-3	2-0	2-1	1-1	1-1	1-0	2-2	0-4		0-0	2-2	1-3	2-0	1-1	1-2	3-1	1-1	1-2	2-4	1-0
Leamington	2-0	1-1	1-1	1-1	4-0	2-0	1-1	1-0	3-0	2-1		1-1	2-1	0-1	0-1	3-0	3-1	3-1	3-0	2-1	1-1
Leiston	2-1	2-1	2-2	1-2	3-1	2-3	1-2	2-1	2-0	0-2	1-1		4-1	0-3	0-0	0-1	2-3	1-1	3-2	0-1	2-0
Long Eaton United	1-6	0-3	2-4	1-1	1-0	0-1	0-6	1-2	1-2	2-2	2-2	2-1		0-5	0-0	0-2	1-3	3-3	1-3	2-2	2-3
Mickleover	5-0	0-1	4-2	2-1	4-0	1-0	1-0	1-0	2-1	4-1	0-0	5-0	5-1		1-1	2-2	2-0	0-5	3-0	2-1	1-1
Needham Market	3-0	2-0	2-0	2-1	3-0	2-1	0-0	0-0	2-0	4-0	2-1	5-0	2-1	0-2		3-0	3-1	6-1	0-3	1-0	1-0
Redditch United	2-1	1-1	1-0	1-2	1-0	1-0	3-4	1-1	3-0	2-0	0-3	5-0	2-0	0-2	3-0		3-1	0-2	1-3	0-1	2-0
Royston Town	2-1	2-2	4-1	0-3	2-2	0-4	2-0	0-1	1-0	4-0	1-0	4-2	3-0	4-1	0-2	1-0		2-4	1-1	1-1	2-3
St Ives Town	1-1	2-3	3-2	3-1	1-0	0-1	1-2	4-2	1-2	6-0	0-1	5-0	5-0	0-2	3-2	2-3	3-2		1-4	4-1	1-3
Stamford	2-2	0-1	0-1	4-0	0-0	2-2	3-1	3-0	2-0	3-2	2-2	3-0	2-0	4-0	0-3	2-2	1-2	4-2		3-0	2-4
Stourbridge	1-1	2-2	1-0	2-0	6-0	1-1	4-2	3-4	0-2	2-1	1-1	1-3	3-0	3-1	1-1	0-1	1-0	2-0	1-1		0-1
Stratford Town	4-2	0-3	3-2	4-3	2-1	1-2	2-1	1-0	0-1	2-0	2-2	3-4	3-2	3-2	6-1	0-1	2-1	1-0	2-1	2-0	

Southern Football League
Premier Division Central

Season 2023/2024

Needham Market	**40**	**26**	**7**	**7**	**74**	**34**	**85**
AFC Telford United	40	24	10	6	69	34	82
Leamington	**40**	**19**	**14**	**7**	**61**	**32**	**71**
Redditch United	40	21	7	12	65	52	70
Mickleover	40	25	6	9	77	43	69
Stratford Town	40	21	6	13	69	57	69
Stamford	40	19	9	12	80	58	66
Halesowen Town	40	18	8	14	54	50	62
St. Ives Town	40	18	4	18	87	72	58
Royston Town	40	17	6	17	63	61	57
Coalville Town	40	15	10	15	68	57	55
Stourbridge	40	14	10	16	52	50	52
Leiston	40	14	10	16	56	71	52
Barwell	40	13	12	15	64	65	51
Kettering Town	40	13	9	18	49	74	48
Alvechurch	40	12	9	19	49	70	45
Bromsgrove Sporting	40	12	8	20	44	51	44
AFC Sudbury	40	10	10	20	53	62	40
Hitchin Town	***40***	***11***	***6***	***23***	***46***	***64***	***39***
Long Eaton United	***40***	***5***	***7***	***28***	***39***	***109***	***22***
Berkhamsted	***40***	***3***	***12***	***25***	***31***	***84***	***21***

Nuneaton Borough resigned from the league during January 2024 and their record was expunged.

Mickleover had 12 points deducted for fielding an ineligible player.

Southern Football League Premier Division South 2023-2024 season	AFC Totton	Basingstoke Town	Beaconsfield Town	Bracknell Town	Chesham United	Didcot Town	Dorchester Town	Gosport Borough	Hanwell Town	Harrow Borough	Hayes & Yeading United	Hendon	Hungerford Town	Merthyr Town	Plymouth Parkway	Poole Town	Salisbury	Sholing	Swindon Supermarine	Tiverton Town	Walton & Hersham	Winchester City
AFC Totton		2-2	3-0	3-2	2-2	7-1	4-4	1-1	5-3	1-0	2-1	1-1	1-2	2-0	2-0	1-0	0-2	1-3	3-1	5-0	3-0	1-1
Basingstoke Town	3-2		1-1	1-3	1-1	2-4	3-1	3-0	1-3	5-0	0-3	3-2	2-2	1-3	1-0	4-2	0-0	1-2	4-3	3-2	3-3	0-2
Beaconsfield Town	0-2	2-3		3-0	1-2	2-1	3-4	1-2	1-0	3-1	2-3	2-2	3-3	0-5	1-1	1-3	0-0	2-1	3-4	2-3	2-1	1-2
Bracknell Town	1-5	4-0	0-3		4-0	5-1	1-3	4-3	3-1	1-1	3-3	1-0	3-1	3-2	2-0	1-1	2-1	5-1	5-0	3-0	3-0	3-1
Chesham United	2-0	2-0	3-0	1-2		1-1	2-0	2-0	1-1	4-0	1-0	2-1	2-1	2-1	4-3	3-1	2-1	2-1	4-0	2-0	3-0	1-2
Didcot Town	0-1	2-3	0-1	1-0	1-1		0-1	0-4	1-3	2-2	0-1	1-2	0-1	1-2	3-2	0-7	1-2	0-1	0-2	0-0	1-1	1-0
Dorchester Town	0-4	4-1	2-1	1-2	0-2	3-1		0-3	2-1	2-2	1-1	2-2	2-4	3-2	0-0	1-2	1-0	1-2	2-1	2-1	1-2	0-4
Gosport Borough	2-0	4-1	1-2	2-0	4-2	0-0	2-2		3-2	1-0	1-2	2-1	4-0	2-1	1-1	1-2	1-1	1-0	1-2	2-1	2-2	2-1
Hanwell Town	0-0	1-2	2-0	1-2	0-3	2-0	1-1	0-0		2-1	1-1	2-2	1-0	1-4	4-0	0-3	2-3	2-3	1-2	1-2	1-2	4-4
Harrow Borough	1-2	4-2	2-1	1-4	1-4	3-3	0-2	2-0	0-3		1-1	1-3	1-6	1-2	2-1	2-4	2-3	3-2	2-2	1-2	1-4	1-2
Hayes & Yeading United	0-1	1-0	1-3	3-2	1-2	1-2	0-1	0-3	1-3	3-0		0-0	3-2	1-1	0-2	5-3	0-2	0-0	2-2	5-2	0-0	1-3
Hendon	3-3	2-0	4-5	1-1	0-1	3-1	1-0	0-0	3-3	2-2	4-3		2-2	1-0	0-2	2-0	0-0	3-1	2-3	2-3	1-1	2-1
Hungerford Town	1-0	1-0	3-1	3-1	0-1	2-2	1-1	0-2	2-2	2-1	3-3	3-0		1-1	7-0	2-1	1-0	2-1	3-2	1-2	0-1	2-2
Merthyr Town	1-3	4-1	2-3	2-3	1-3	4-0	3-2	1-4	4-0	7-1	1-1	1-1	3-0		1-1	0-2	2-1	2-1	4-1	2-1	1-1	1-2
Plymouth Parkway	0-3	1-1	0-1	1-0	4-0	2-1	5-0	0-2	1-2	1-3	3-1	3-0	6-2	1-3		1-0	0-1	1-3	4-1	1-1	2-2	1-1
Poole Town	0-0	0-1	3-0	3-1	2-5	2-0	1-2	2-0	0-3	1-0	0-2	2-2	1-2	1-3	2-2		4-5	0-3	1-0	2-0	1-3	2-1
Salisbury	0-1	2-1	1-1	2-0	3-1	2-2	3-2	2-0	2-0	0-2	2-1	2-1	2-1	0-0	2-1	2-0		3-0	3-2	4-2	1-0	2-2
Sholing	0-0	0-4	0-0	0-0	0-1	2-2	1-2	0-3	1-1	1-3	1-0	2-2	3-3	0-2	1-1	2-0	2-1		3-0	0-4	0-1	5-1
Swindon Supermarine	2-2	3-0	3-3	3-1	2-1	4-1	1-2	0-2	1-1	1-3	3-2	0-1	2-3	0-3	3-0	2-7	3-3	0-0		2-2	2-1	3-0
Tiverton Town	1-2	2-2	2-2	2-1	2-0	5-3	0-2	1-2	2-0	0-0	1-1	2-4	0-1	2-0	2-2	4-2	1-3	1-0	1-1		2-2	2-0
Walton & Hersham	2-2	1-2	1-0	5-2	2-2	4-2	6-3	0-4	1-2	4-4	2-0	1-3	4-1	2-3	1-2	3-0	1-0	1-0	4-2	2-0		3-1
Winchester City	0-6	2-1	1-0	5-0	0-3	1-2	1-1	1-1	1-1	1-2	1-1	0-2	1-0	2-0	1-1	4-0	1-1	1-3	2-2	2-1	2-1	

Southern Football League
Premier Division South

Season 2023/2024

Chesham United	**42**	**28**	**6**	**8**	**83**	**46**	**90**
AFC Totton	42	23	12	7	89	45	81
Salisbury	**42**	**23**	**10**	**9**	**70**	**46**	**79**
Gosport Borough	42	23	9	10	75	43	78
Bracknell Town	42	21	5	16	84	71	68
Merthyr Town	42	20	7	15	85	59	67
Walton & Hersham	42	18	11	13	78	67	65
Hungerford Town	42	18	10	14	77	70	64
Dorchester Town	42	17	9	16	66	77	60
Hendon	42	14	16	12	70	65	58
Winchester City	42	15	12	15	63	67	57
Basingstoke Town	42	15	8	19	69	83	53
Poole Town	42	16	4	22	70	76	52
Tiverton Town	42	14	10	18	64	74	52
Sholing	42	13	10	19	52	63	49
Swindon Supermarine	42	13	10	19	73	92	49
Hanwell Town	42	12	12	18	64	71	48
Plymouth Parkway	42	12	12	18	60	68	48
Beaconsfield Town	***42***	***13***	***9***	***20***	***63***	***78***	***48***
Hayes & Yeading United	***42***	***11***	***13***	***18***	***59***	***67***	***46***
Harrow Borough	***42***	***10***	***9***	***23***	***60***	***97***	***39***
Didcot Town	***42***	***6***	***10***	***26***	***45***	***94***	***28***

Southern Football League Division One Central 2023-2024 season	AFC Dunstable	Aylesbury United	Barton Rovers	Bedford Town	Biggleswade	Biggleswade Town	Cirencester Town	Hadley	Hertford Town	Kempston Rovers	Kidlington	Kings Langley	Leighton Town	North Leigh	Stotfold	Thame United	Waltham Abbey	Ware	Welwyn Garden City
AFC Dunstable		1-2	4-0	1-3	3-2	1-0	2-3	2-1	4-1	2-1	2-0	5-6	4-4	2-4	2-0	2-1	2-5	1-3	1-0
Aylesbury United	2-1		0-4	0-0	1-0	1-3	1-3	2-3	1-2	0-0	2-2	1-2	2-4	2-0	4-4	1-2	3-2	0-0	3-2
Barton Rovers	3-0	4-2		0-0	1-2	0-3	1-3	5-2	2-1	2-2	1-4	3-3	2-0	1-1	0-3	2-2	0-0	2-1	3-2
Bedford Town	0-3	1-2	2-0		2-1	2-3	3-1	2-3	7-0	2-0	5-1	1-1	1-1	4-0	1-1	3-2	0-1	7-1	5-1
Biggleswade	2-3	2-0	2-2	2-2		1-2	1-1	4-3	1-2	4-1	1-1	2-0	1-2	1-2	3-1	0-2	0-1	4-0	4-5
Biggleswade Town	2-2	2-1	3-2	0-1	2-0		1-2	2-2	2-3	0-1	3-1	2-0	1-1	3-0	3-3	1-0	2-3	4-1	4-3
Cirencester Town	2-2	2-1	3-0	1-1	1-2	1-4		3-0	3-1	4-0	0-1	1-1	2-2	3-0	2-2	3-0	4-1	0-1	3-0
Hadley	1-0	1-2	1-3	0-1	2-1	0-2	1-0		3-1	1-0	0-3	2-1	0-1	6-0	2-1	3-0	4-3	0-0	3-2
Hertford Town	1-2	2-2	0-0	0-2	2-0	2-2	2-3	4-2		3-1	1-1	4-2	1-3	2-1	1-3	5-1	2-1	0-2	1-2
Kempston Rovers	0-2	0-5	2-2	2-1	1-3	0-3	1-3	1-6	1-4		0-0	0-3	2-0	1-2	1-4	1-0	0-0	4-2	1-2
Kidlington	2-3	3-1	1-0	1-1	1-2	0-4	4-3	0-0	2-0	0-1		2-2	4-1	4-2	1-3	2-1	3-3	1-0	0-2
Kings Langley	4-2	2-0	2-2	1-3	1-2	2-2	1-1	1-1	1-0	6-2	4-2		0-3	5-1	2-2	3-1	1-2	4-1	2-4
Leighton Town	1-2	4-1	2-0	0-2	0-2	0-1	0-0	1-2	3-2	1-3	1-0	0-1		1-2	5-1	3-1	0-0	0-4	1-4
North Leigh	3-0	2-3	3-4	1-4	0-3	0-4	2-1	0-2	1-3	0-2	3-0	4-1	3-0		1-4	3-0	1-0	1-3	1-2
Stotfold	0-1	4-3	1-0	0-2	6-0	1-3	2-1	2-0	5-0	2-1	1-0	2-1	2-0	0-2		0-2	0-2	1-1	3-1
Thame United	3-3	3-1	1-3	1-2	1-1	1-0	0-2	2-1	0-1	1-0	1-2	3-0	1-3	3-0	2-1		2-4	1-3	0-1
Waltham Abbey	2-6	2-3	1-1	0-0	1-1	1-0	1-0	2-3	5-1	3-1	2-0	2-4	2-1	4-0	2-1	3-2		4-1	1-4
Ware	1-2	2-3	3-1	4-2	1-0	0-1	1-0	4-2	1-0	3-0	2-0	3-0	5-1	1-3	1-1	4-4	1-0		4-2
Welwyn Garden City	1-2	3-3	3-2	1-3	2-5	0-3	1-1	2-1	0-0	4-2	2-0	6-1	2-1	1-3	3-0	3-4	1-4	5-4	

Southern Football League Division One Central

Season 2023/2024

Biggleswade Town	**36**	**22**	**6**	**8**	**77**	**39**	**72**
Bedford Town	**36**	**20**	**9**	**7**	**78**	**37**	**69**
AFC Dunstable	36	20	4	12	77	66	64
Waltham Abbey	36	18	7	11	70	55	61
Ware	36	18	5	13	69	61	59
Cirencester Town	36	16	9	11	66	44	57
Stotfold	36	16	7	13	67	56	55
Hadley	36	17	4	15	64	60	55
Welwyn Garden City	36	17	3	16	79	79	54
Biggleswade	36	14	6	16	62	58	48
Kings Langley	36	13	9	14	71	74	48
Barton Rovers	36	11	11	14	58	65	44
Kidlington	36	12	8	16	49	60	44
Hertford Town	36	13	5	18	55	73	44
Aylesbury United	36	12	7	17	61	74	43
North Leigh	36	14	1	21	52	80	43
Leighton Town	36	12	6	18	51	62	42
Thame United	***36***	***11***	***4***	***21***	***51***	***70***	***37***
Kempston Rovers	***36***	***8***	***5***	***23***	***36***	***80***	***29***

Southern Football League Division One South 2023-2024 season	Bashley	Bemerton Heath Harlequins	Bideford	Bishops Cleeve	Bristol Manor Farm	Cribbs	Evesham United	Exmouth Town	Frome Town	Larkhall Athletic	Malvern Town	Melksham Town	Mousehole AFC	Paulton Rovers	Tavistock	Westbury United	Willand Rovers	Wimborne Town	Yate Town
Bashley		2-3	1-3	0-2	0-1	0-3	1-1	1-2	3-2	1-3	1-2	1-2	2-0	4-1	0-0	1-1	3-2	1-2	2-0
Bemerton Heath Harlequins	2-4		2-0	1-2	4-2	0-2	0-5	0-3	3-1	2-1	0-4	2-2	1-2	0-0	2-1	1-1	4-2	0-0	4-0
Bideford	1-3	1-1		4-1	1-1	1-2	0-2	2-1	0-1	2-1	3-1	3-1	1-1	0-0	2-3	0-3	0-2	3-1	1-1
Bishops Cleeve	1-1	2-0	0-1		0-2	2-2	3-0	1-4	2-2	4-0	0-0	6-1	4-1	6-2	3-4	3-2	0-0	2-5	2-2
Bristol Manor Farm	0-0	4-0	2-3	1-1		3-1	2-0	3-2	1-2	2-2	3-1	3-0	3-4	0-3	2-3	2-0	3-0	1-2	1-1
Cribbs	2-2	1-0	2-0	0-4	1-0		0-0	1-0	1-0	1-1	2-1	1-0	1-2	1-0	2-2	1-0	1-1	2-1	2-1
Evesham United	2-0	2-1	1-2	1-0	1-2	1-1		2-4	2-3	0-0	0-2	5-3	1-2	0-0	3-1	0-0	3-2	0-0	1-1
Exmouth Town	0-1	0-4	0-1	1-1	2-3	2-3	1-1		0-0	5-0	1-3	2-1	2-2	1-2	0-1	1-1	3-1	1-4	1-2
Frome Town	2-1	3-0	4-0	1-0	3-3	0-0	3-2	2-1		2-0	4-0	2-2	1-0	1-0	3-1	3-1	3-0	2-2	2-0
Larkhall Athletic	2-0	1-2	4-3	1-3	1-3	5-1	1-1	5-0	1-1		2-0	1-0	1-0	4-0	3-0	1-0	2-1	3-1	2-2
Malvern Town	6-0	3-1	2-2	2-0	1-0	1-3	2-3	3-0	1-3	2-4		1-1	2-1	2-2	2-1	0-3	3-0	1-2	0-0
Melksham Town	0-0	4-0	2-1	1-0	2-2	2-3	1-1	2-0	1-2	1-5	2-2		3-2	5-0	0-1	0-2	0-0	1-3	0-3
Mousehole AFC	2-2	3-1	5-0	7-3	2-0	2-2	1-3	4-1	3-2	1-1	3-0	3-4		3-0	3-2	4-0	4-0	1-3	0-1
Paulton Rovers	1-2	4-4	0-1	2-4	1-3	0-1	1-1	2-1	2-7	0-1	2-2	0-1	3-3		0-2	0-1	1-0	0-2	1-0
Tavistock	2-3	1-2	1-2	3-1	0-2	5-4	1-3	0-2	6-2	3-3	2-0	1-1	2-2	2-1		0-0	1-3	3-2	1-1
Westbury United	2-0	2-0	0-0	4-4	0-4	0-0	0-1	0-2	2-3	1-1	5-3	1-4	0-4	3-4	2-3		2-3	3-2	0-2
Willand Rovers	0-2	2-4	2-1	4-0	1-2	2-1	3-1	3-1	0-0	2-2	1-1	0-0	2-1	5-1	2-0	0-0		0-1	2-2
Wimborne Town	4-0	1-1	3-1	1-0	4-0	2-2	2-1	1-1	1-1	2-1	2-0	2-1	3-2	2-1	3-2	3-2	4-2		1-0
Yate Town	0-0	3-0	1-0	0-1	1-1	3-3	1-5	4-1	0-1	4-1	2-3	4-1	1-2	3-0	5-1	2-1	3-0	0-2	

Southern Football League Division One South

Season 2023/2024

Wimborne Town	**36**	**24**	**7**	**5**	**76**	**42**	**79**
Frome Town	**36**	**22**	**9**	**5**	**74**	**42**	**75**
Cribbs	36	18	12	6	56	46	66
Bristol Manor Farm	36	17	8	11	67	50	59
Mousehole	36	17	7	12	82	58	58
Larkhall Athletic	36	16	10	10	67	53	58
Evesham United	36	13	12	11	56	47	51
Yate Town	36	13	11	12	56	46	50
Bishop's Cleeve	36	13	9	14	68	63	48
Malvern Town	36	13	8	15	59	61	47
Tavistock	36	13	7	16	62	71	46
Bideford	36	13	7	16	46	58	46
Bemerton Heath Harlequins	36	12	7	17	52	71	43
Willand Rovers	36	11	9	16	50	60	42
Bashley	36	11	9	16	45	59	42
Melksham Town	36	10	10	16	52	65	40
Westbury United	36	8	10	18	45	62	34
Exmouth Town	36	9	6	21	49	67	33
Paulton Rovers	***36***	***6***	***8***	***22***	***37***	***78***	***26***

Hamworthy United resigned from the league on 6th October 2023 and their record was expunged: 7 1 2 4 10 16 5